Anonymous

Utah Statehood

Reasons why it should not be granted. Will the American people surrender

the territory to an unscrupulous and polygamous theocracy? Embracing:

The Mormon preliminary movement.

.

Anonymous

Utah Statehood
*Reasons why it should not be granted. Will the American people surrender the
territory to an unscrupulous and polygamous theocracy? Embracing: The Mormon
preliminary movement.*

ISBN/EAN: 9783337295424

Printed in Europe, USA, Canada, Australia, Japan

Cover: Foto ©Suzi / pixelio.de

More available books at **www.hansebooks.com**

UTAH STATEHOOD.

Reasons Why it Should Not be Granted.

WILL THE AMERICAN PEOPLE SURRENDER THE TERRITORY TO AN UNSCRUPULOUS AND POLYGAMOUS THEOCRACY?

EMBRACING:

The Mormon Preliminary Movement; the Democratic and Republican Refusal to Take Part and Their Reasons Therefor; Utah Commission Report; Governor West in Opposition; Review of the Proposed Mormon Constitution; Its Failure to Meet the Requirements of the Occasion.

SALT LAKE CITY:
TRIBUNE PRINT.

1887.

THE MOVEMENT FOR STATEHOOD.

On the 17th of June, 1887, a proposition for a Constitutional Convention and an application to Congress for the admission of the Territory as a State was suddenly sprung in Utah. Its initial step was the call for the Convention; this was presently followed by a proposition by what is locally known as the "People's Party" to the Democratic and Republican organizations in the Territory, soliciting their co-operation in the movement, and offering to accord them a "fair representation in the Convention." This proposition was declined by them, for reasons which fully appear in the correspondence appended hereto.

According to the plan, "mass conventions" were held in the several counties, delegates were chosen by acclamation, without regard to the forms of election or qualification of voters, in about one week, and the Convention assembled on the 30th and went through the form of adopting a Constitution, with some provisions designed to disarm opposition, which are utter failures, if not satisfactory.

The non Mormon population of the Territory, of both National parties, as a body, declined to participate in the "mass conventions," or in the proceedings of the Convention; but united in a body as the Liberal Party of the Territory in opposition to the politico-religious rule of the dominant sect; they held a Territorial Convention which adopted resolutions declining to take part in the movement, for the reasons which are therein stated, the same being hereto annexed.

In taking this position, the non-Mormons of the Territory were thoroughly impressed by their experience and an intimate knowledge of the spirit and methods of the dominant sect, that the admission of the Territory as a State under control of this bitter sectarianism would be destructive to their personal rights and material interests, the measure of protection now enjoyed under national supervision being withdrawn. They do not believe that there is any real intention on the part of the Mormons to abandon or punish the crime of polygamy, or to renounce political control by ecclesiastical organization, but are firmly convinced that the principal purpose of the movement is to entrench both under the power of a State, untrammeled by National laws.

To show that their apprehensions are well founded, a brief reference may be made to the history of the Territory and to the methods of the Mormon Church, which is a most thorough organization for political not less than for so-called religious purposes. The lust for political power and its abuse have been characteristic of the political branch of the Mormon Church which has appropriated the Territory of Utah. Merely premising the uniform results of their contact with the States of Ohio, Missouri and Illinois, brief mention may be made of a few facts in the history of Utah under Mormon rule in its relation to the Nation.

At the first, the office of Governor, by a mistaken policy, was put in the hands of the head of the Church, and the political power of the Territory was wholly surrendered to its control. Thus intrenched, its Legislature embarked in a scheme to secure to the Territory complete autonomy; it established the Mormon Church, an independent military organization and an independent judiciary, in defiance of the Organic Act; organized a corporation with unprecedented powers and privileges, made fraudulent grants of public land to carry out a gigantic system of pauper immigration of converts, and provided by special grants and general regulation for engrossing the public land, timber and water in the Territory, so as to exclude "outsiders"—all this under the claim of a State government disguised as a Territory.

Having thus substantially an Independent government, the next step was to drive out the judges and get up a rebellion without a single grievance; a general pardon from the President was received as an "intervention of Providence," and the Government and people of the United States have been, from that day to the present, regarded by them as enemies of "this people."

The judiciary system being thus disorganized by the illegal acts of the local Legislature, all jurisdiction, criminal and civil, continued to be exercised by the local courts, and the judges appointed by the President were idle spectators, till Congress finally interfered, and, by the Poland Act in 1874, disapproved of these illegal local acts and settled the jurisdiction of the various grades of courts. But that act introduced a vice into the jury system by granting to a Mormon agent the power to select half the panel from which all juries were to be drawn. It was not surprising that this concession rendered the execution of the law a farce in all cases where the law was distasteful to the Mormons. This judicial paralysis continued until 1884, when it was decided by a District Court, and affirmed by the Territorial and United States Supreme Courts, that the District Courts were not confined to the panel of 200 jurors thus selected, but, when that panel was exhausted, might resort to an open venire. This decision put the laws into effect in 1884, and it, applied in the enforcement of the Edmunds act of 1882, has, during the last three years, put into successful operation the National laws which are distasteful to the Mormons. The result was that the chief leaders of the Church absconded or went into concealment, aided and abetted by the body of the Mormon people, and a large number of lesser note have been convicted of church crimes and confined in the Penitentiary, after having rejected the offer, by the Courts, of freedom from that punishment on the mild condition of a promise on their part to obey the law in future.

At length, being brought face to face with law, the Mormon power in Utah, has resorted to two expedients, which are wholly inconsistent, in order to secure relief from the predicament: the first was a bold defiance of the law and decisions of courts in the name and pretext of religion; the other was a subterfuge of an equivocal declaration by which they offer to enforce law against what they claim as religion, on condition that Congress shall emancipate them from National control and invest them with the powers of a State.

At a General Conference of the Mormon Church held at Logan on the 6th of May, 1885, it was unanimously resolved "that a committee be appointed to draft a series of resolutions and a protest to the President of the United States, and to the Nation," and to report the same to a mass meeting to be afterwards called. A committee of twenty-two (of which Hon. John T. Caine, present Delegate to Congress from Utah was chairman) was appointed. They prepared an address and protest accordingly, which was submitted to mass meetings called in the several counties in the Territory on May 2, 1885, and by each of these meetings was unanimously adopted, and said Caine was deputed as the agent of the Mormon Church and party to present the address and protest to the President and Nation. This document thus had the most formal and positive endorsement of the Mormon Church and "People's Party," and may be taken as the deliberate expression of their convictions and determinations as to the issue which they had forced on the Nation by opposition to its laws. This address arraigns the Government and the courts for persecution because of the execution of the laws against polygamy and unlawful cohabitation, and among other things makes the following deliberate declaration:

"Among the principles of our religion is that of immediate revelation from God; one of the doctrines so revealed is celestial or plural m-rriage, for which ostensibly we are stigmatized and hated. This is a vital part of our religion, the decisions of courts to the contrary notwithstanding. Even the Utah Commission concede this. In their report to the Secretary of the

— 5 —

Interior, November, 1884, speaking of plural marriage, they say: 'This article of their faith is as much an essential and substantial part of their creed, as their belief in baptism, repentance for the forgiveness of sins, and the like. * * * All orthodox Mormons believe polygamy to be right, and that it is an essential part of their creed.'"

This address failed to have its desired effect upon the Nation; prosecutions and convictions went on and defiance of the laws under pretext of religion continued, until Congress found it necessary to enact further and more stringent provisions to suppress the inveterate evils, and the Edmunds-Tucker act of March 3, 1887, was passed. The passage of a much more stringent bill by the House created widespread consternation in Utah, because it proposed to withdraw, in large measure, political power from hands which had always used it to defeat and nullify the National laws.

Thus the issue in Utah was narrowed down to this alternative: the Mormons must either submit to the law, or find some road out of the predicament. They chose the latter. While they are still defying the National laws, the expedient of a Constitutional Convention and an application for Statehood was adopted, under duress of the situation.

Now, as to the proposed Constitution: In view of the deliberate, formal and unanimous declaration of the Mormon people made only two years ago, that polygamy is a vital part of their religion, can the equivocal and suspicious declaration in Sec. 11, Art. 15, be considered as made in good faith and with an honest purpose to carry it into execution? If the declarations in the unanimous address of 1885 were sincere, this provision in the Constitution is a shallow and contemptible pretence; and if this Constitutional provision was intended as the expression of an honest purpose to abandon and suppress the crime of polygamy, then the address of 1885 is a play of hypocrisy and fraud to cloak crime: and the Hon. John T. Caine, Delegate in Congress, who signed and presented the address and who presided over the Convention and subscribed the proposed Constitution, has spitted himself on the horns of this dilemma, as a spectacle for the Nation.

Section 12 of article 15 of the proposed Constitution is as follows:

SEC. 12. Bigamy and polygamy being considered incompatible with a republican form of government, each of them is hereby forbidden and declared a misdemeanor. Any person who shall violate this section shall, on conviction thereof, be punished by a fine of not more than one thousand dollars and be imprisoned for a term of not less than six months nor more than three years, in the discretion of the court. This section shall be construed as operative without the aid of legislation, and the offenses prohibited by this section shall not be barred by any statute of limitation within three years after the commission of the offense; nor shall the power of pardon be extended thereto until such pardon shall be approved by the President of the United states.

This extraordinary effort of statesmanship presents the anomaly of a penal statute and a statute of limitation combined, and proposes such a union of Federal and State legislation and executive functions as no wisdom had hitherto conceived. There is no minimum limit of the fine and it may be one cent. The crime is a mere misdemeanor, and being so classified in the constitution, no future legislature could declare or punish it as a felony. No disability is annexed to a conviction, and persons committing the crime in future or continuing in their present criminal relations, could vote and hold offices in the proposed State. Conviction of treason and felony alone deprives the accused of the privileges of an elector; and all burden is taken from the shoulders of the Legislature of the State in providing for the enforcement of this provision—it is to be self-operative without the aid of legislation, and it might as well be further provided, without the aid of courts, judges, prosecutors, or juries, for it is not within the scope of probabilities that an organized community, which claims that these crimes are a "vital part" of their religion, will now enforce this provision. It is an empty promise, but half made, and designed to mislead. Up to this day this whole Mormon community, with united voice, assail the government and its courts with loud accusations of persecution for executing National laws against these very crimes.

The non-Mormons of Utah do not believe that the application for Statehood is made in good faith, or with any purpose of abandoning polygamy or of even punishing it; but it is their unanimous opinion that the admission of Utah as a State under control of the Mormon political party would result, first in loss of their personal rights and property, and, second, in an inevitable conflict with the Federal Government.

The Mormons are a law to themselves, and respect no law which does not suit them, or which may conflict with their pretended revelations. They have never kept faith with any government or party. They have rejected all overtures of Congress designed to lead them to a respect for its laws and to impress them with its clemency. When allowed an appeal to the United States Supreme Court on convictions for polygamy, it was in hope on the one side, and an implied promise on the other, that the final decision would be respected and the law thereafter obeyed: but a decision sustaining the constitutionality of the law was overturned and the crime ran riot, "the decisions of the courts to the contrary notwithstanding." When all the fruits of the crime born prior to January, 1883, were legitimated by act of Congress, in answer to pitiful appeals in their behalf, it was in the hope on the part of Congress, and upon an implied promise on the part of the Mormons, that they cease the adulteration of population thereafter; but the same result followed—the evil has gone on in its wide-spreading circles—and this concession was made the basis of a further claim which was urged before the courts to defeat the law against unlawful cohabitation, viz., that Congress having legitimated their children, it could not rightly claim that the fathers should not continue the marital relation with their mothers. When given the power to draw half the panel of jurors, they exercised the same to defeat the execution of the laws, and their organs with a sense of security, said in derision to the officers of the law, "Now you have the courts and the law, why don't you execute it?" and people talked of the "Mormon problem" as something insoluble. But three years of practical operation of the laws, though against many obstacles interposed (among which is frequent and shameless perjury) has produced the present crisis in Utah. The Mormons seek Statehood to get out of the dilemma without submitting to the law; the non-Mormons of Utah appeal to Congress not to deliver them over to a majority which treats all others as enemies. These ask that Congress continue the ægis of its protection over them until Utah is brought into harmony with free and civilized institutions, and that the National laws be continued in force to that end; that, if the obstinate and continued evils shall render it necessary, such laws may be so amended and extended to reach and entirely suppress the evils; and, especially, that delegated political power may be withdrawn where it is used to nullify the National laws and fortify these inveterate evils.

The Mormon power is utterly irreconcilable with and repugnant to all civil government: in its aspirations and its maxims, or dogmas, it is subversive of all governments but its own. It is anti-republican and essentially monarchical in its organization, and is characterized by the feature of a few schemers who command, a large ignorant mass who obey, and these are not the elements out of which a free State can be created.

At the Territorial election held in August, 1887, the Mormons or "People's Party" voted almost unanimously to ratify the so-called constitution, (as appears by an unofficial count), but the Gentiles or non-Mormons, as a body, declined to vote on the question. The latter, however, of both National parties, united as the Liberal party, made nominations for District and County officers, and succeeded in electing four members of the Legislature. A short time before, by a like united effort, they had succeeded in electing school trustees in three or four of the school districts of Salt Lake City. Civilization has begun to move in Utah, though its progress is slow. Admit the Territory as a State, and retrogression will succeed, and the said "vital principle" and all "essential parts" of the Mormon creed will find free action, without restraint of law, and the minorty will be abandoned without its protections; and after all the Nation will have a more aggravated "Utah question" to settle behind a State Constitution.

THE MORMON INVITATION AND THE GENTILE REPLY,

The following correspondence is self-explanatory:

HEADQUARTERS PEOPLE'S
TERRITORIAL CENTRAL COMMITTEE,
SALT LAKE CITY, UTAH, June 17, 1887.

J. B. Rosborough, Esq., Chairman Central Committee, Democratic Party of Utah, Salt Lake City, Utah:—DEAR SIR—The Territorial Central Committee of the People's Party, considering that the time is propitious for an application for admission into the Union, of the Territory of Utah, has called mass conventions, to be held in the several counties, June 25th, to nominate delegates to a Constitutional Convention to be held in this city June 30, 1887. It is desired that this movement be made as general as possible, and that all classes of the people of the Territory shall participate in it. We therefore solicit the co-operation of the Democratic Party of Utah, and through you as its chairman, we respectfully invite your committee and your party, to take an active part in the mass conventions, and to assist in the nomination of delegates to the Constitutional Convention, with the understanding that if you accept this invitation, your party shall be accorded a fair representation in the convention.

By order of the People's Territorial Central Committee.   JOHN R. WINDER, Chairman.

JUNIUS WELLS, Cor. Secretary.

ON BEHALF OF THE DEMOCRATS.

CHAIRMAN ROSBOROUGH'S REPLY.

SALT LAKE CITY, June 24, 1887.

John R. Winder. Esq., Chairman People's Territorial Central Committee:—DEAR SIR:— I have the honor to acknowledge the receipt on Sunday the 18th inst., of your favor of the 17th inst., announcing that your committee had called "mass conventions" to meet in the several counties on the 25th inst., to nominate delegates to a Constitutional Convention to be held in this city on the 30th inst., and inviting the co-operation of the Democratic Party of Utah in the movement, with the understanding that they will be accorded "a fair representation," in such convention.

Having determined the propriety of the measure and taken action, you ask our co-operation. The brief interval of less than a week, has precluded the possibility of getting our committee together, to consider and answer in a more formal manner your proposal, or present to you such counter-proposal as is hereinafter indicated, looking to a previous consideration and discussion of the propriety and expediency of such a movement under existing conditions in the Territory.

Your proposition, in plain words, is that the Democrats in the Territory unite with you in asking Congress to retire from the issue forced upon the Federal Government by opposition to its laws maintained by the dominant party in the Territory, and invest Utah, under the continued domination of that party reinforced by its lately disfranchised members with the powers of State Government. Now, so far as I know, there is not a Democrat, or, as for that matter, a single non-Mormon of any shade of political faith in Utah, who is willing to co-operate in the proposed measure, or would not regard its consummation as not only destructive of their individual rights and interests, but suicidal to the peace and prosperity of the Territory. A long residence here, and a familiarity with the discussions elicited by the abnormal condition of affairs in Utah, have impressed me with a sense of the unanimity of that opinion and belief, and the reasons therefor. In giving expression to the same and of

THEIR UNWILLINGNESS TO JOIN

in your design of a State Government, it is proper that I should here state some of these reasons in order that the same may be better understood, and that the country may judge, whether the time is "propitious" or the Territory prepared for Statehood.

1. It is the duty of Congress to secure to the several States in the Union, a Government, Republican in fact and in spirit, as well as in form, and this obligation imposes the further duty of seeing, before the admission of any new State, that its people are prepared for the safe exercise of State control, and in harmony with our political institutions. Utah under the control of your party, invested with delegated powers, has stood, for a quarter of a century, and still stands, arrayed against National laws, and used these delegated powers to defeat their operation.

2. Your party is the dominant church, and that church, as a political organization, constitutes your party; nothing contained in one, is wanting in the other, and neither contains

what is not tolerated in the other: they are one and the same in their membership, so that independent political action by an indi_vidual, can never occur except with apostacy from the cre:d. The theory upon which our republican institutions are based, is that all political power is derived from the people. On the contrary the leaders of your party, claim and teach, and their followers concede that all rightful political power is derived from God, and is delegated to his chosen ministers, who have a divine commission to rule over the people, whose first duty is to obey counsel (i. e., submit to dictation) in temporal as well as spiritual concerns; and they further hold and teach, as a political maxim, as well as a dogma of a creed, that this divine commission entitles them to the present right to, and the near future possession of universal sovereignty to be founded upon the ruins of all secular, (" man made") governments. Such assumptions are utterly repugnant to American institutions, but at the same time these pretentions gauge the patriotism of these leaders and denote the intelligence and other qualifications of their followers for citizenship and Statehood.

3. The assumption of political power under ecclesiastical organization has been the chief cause of the troubles in which

YOUR PARTY HAS BEEN INVOLVED

Wherever in contact with State governments in former times, as in the States of Ohio, Missouri and Illinois, and with Federal authority in Utah. Not satisfied with taking equal chances under the law, with other religious sects, your party adopted, and has always pursued the policy in these States, and later in Utah, of gathering their followers together in compact bodies, organized to act as a unit, in an Ishmaelitish spirit, for the purpose of securing and holding political control. A convincing proof of this fact, is that a branch of your faith, which early repudiated those ambitious purposes, is scattered in many States, in the enjoyment of undis turbed peace. If, clothed with the powers of a sovereign State, an organization which has defied the laws of States and waged a contest with the Government of the United States in opposition to its laws, and in disregard of decisions of the Supreme Court, with the limited powers of a Territory, cannot be trusted to forego the use of those largely increased powers in the same direction, and in such manner and spirit as must necessarily lead to collision with the Federal Government. In the very nature of things, this would be inevitable; and instead of settling the vexed Utah question fi-

nally and peaceably, the admission of the Territory as a State would enlarge and embitter the contest, and render more destructive and deplorable the mode of final settlement.

4. The hasty and irregular mode you have adopted without any enabling act, without consideration or discussion, without the formality of election of delegates, where elective franchise is restricted and qualified, and without any popular demand, is objectionable, and would tend to defeat the purpose of the movement, even if more serious objection did not exist. After more than thirty years of abuse of delegated, legislative and judicial powers by the Territory, Congress in 1882 and again in 1887, revoked some of these powers and vested them in Federal agencies with the express declaration in each of these acts, that such revok-d powers should be withheld, until the Territory by fair and appropriate legislation, should provide for the proper exercise of those powers. Five years have elapsed, and Utah has made no provision

TO MEET THE FAIR OFFER,

But on the contrary, has continued to the present time a factious and unremitting contest with the Federal authority.

Can it, with any reason, be expected that Congress will acknowledge defeat and retire from the contest, and vest in such hands the immense increase of power demanded?

In view of the history and condition of Utah in its political relation to the Federal Government, and the spirit of opposition to its laws, if there ever was a reason for an enabling act, according to usage, in any instance, this Territory presents the most conspicuous case for such prerequisite.

5. No matter what provision or guarantees you may put in your Constitution, there can be no assurance that the powers of a State Government, if conceded, would not be perverted and abused by unfriendly and proscriptive legislation, and by an equally vicious adm nistration, to the extent of driving the hope less minority from the State as "cursed outsiders," as non-Mormons, citizens of the United States, are usually designated in fash ionable pulpit oratory. Constitutional declarations require legislative enactments to put them in force, and these require judicial and ministerial action to give them effect. These functions would be committed to the covenant bound men of your party, reinforced by their associates now disfranchised, in exile or in prison, (the "elite" of the Territory, as they are styled by one chief among them) who maintain that existing laws on like subjects are contrary to the commands or li-

cense of divine revelations, and therefore void. And besides, in a progressive creed, like that of your party, which claims cumulative new revelations from time to time, there may be room and occasion for abrogating Constitutional provisions in obedience to emanations of this kind. Any way, Constitutional guaranties have no force with a majority who consider them null, as opposed to "higher law," or "divine revelation."

6. A most serious apprehension exists in the minds of all non-Mormon people in Utah as to what would be the condition and destiny in store for them if subjected to the unrestricted power of the dominant major ty who are not a homogeneous American population, such as exists in other Territories and States. A very large population has been recruited from the countries of the Old World, with little knowledge and less interest in our republican ideas, history and institutions, but has come or been brought here by assisted immigration for the purpose of building up a temporal kingdom and are thoroughly imbued by sinister teaching with the idea that the people and Government of the United States are their enemies. From the beginning systematic efforts have been employed by the dominant majority to discourage and deter non-Mormon American citizens from settling in Utah, and such as have come here have been

CONSTANTLY BOYCOTTED IN THEIR BUSINESS.

They have been misrepresented and maligned as adventurers seeking to rob Mormons of their property. By pre-occupation under bounty of the Government and by reason of unfriendly neighborhood deterring settlement by others, the dominant sect obtained and hold substantially all rural property suitable for agriculture. Yet the non-Mormons of the Territory, by the enterprise and capital they have brought here, have opened the mines and developed therefrom within the last seventeen years, more than ninety millions of dollars, have expended hundreds of thousands of dollars annually in wages paid to Mormon laborers without distinction, and furnished markets for their agricultural products before a drug, purchased and improved city property and contribute at least one third of the taxes paid. Before the development of this wealth, though the Territory had been settled twenty-three years, its entire annual revenues did not exceed $20,000 and the Territory had

no hospital or asylum or college or system of common schools. Men who have accomplished so much insist upon an equal protection of the law and the mode of its administration which a knowledge of the past warrants them in doubting, should the Territory be admitted as a State.

7. The movement for State Government is premature; if your organization will first prove by their conduct and acts that they recognize the supremacy and binding force of National laws confirmed by judicial scrutiny, without further evasions or obstructions, and end this state of chronic semi-rebellion (as you can easily do, if you mean peace under a State), you can show to Congress convincing evidence of good fa th and a fair claim to the boon of Statehood, without which your proposed application should meet the fate of its several predecessors.

8. Considering that a compliance with your invitation to co-operate with your party in the proposed step would lend to it the specious appearance of being a spontaneous movement originating with the people at large, including all classes, we prefer to leave its management and fortunes to you alone, pending the unsettled contest between your party and the Government, while we appeal to the sense and magnanimity of the nation, to avert what we sincerely believe would, under existing circumstances and conditions here, prove a ruinous calamity.

But after conferring with such of our committee as could be reached in the brief time you allow, I am authorized by them to say to you, that if you will suspend your proposed action and call public meetings at some dates mutually agreed upon, to discuss the propriety of calling a constitutional convention under the usual forms, and whether the time is "propituous" or the people of the Territory prepared to exercise the powers and rights of a sovereign State and will concede the representation you mention, delegates named as our committee may propose, will attend such public meetings and discuss with you those questions, at which time we will undertake to show from the record and history of your own party written by your own leaders, and by other evidence proof of the truth of the facts herein aforesaid, as reasons why Utah should not seek or be accorded Statehood under existing conditions. Respectfully,

J. B. ROSBOROUGH,
Chairman Dem. Ter. Com.

ON BEHALF OF THE REPUBLICANS.

The following is the reply of the Territorial Republican Committee to an invitation from Mr. Winder of the "People's" committee, identical with that sent to Judge Rosborough, and made introductory to his reply elsewhere given:

SALT LAKE CITY, June 24, 1887.

John R. Winder, Esq., Chairman of People's Party Territorial Central Committe, Salt Lake City, Utah:—DEAR SIR:—Your letter addressed to the chairman of the Republican Central Committee, was not received until three days since, by reason of his temporary absence, and the brief time since, has precluded consultation among the entire committee, but having had a meeting of a majority for the purpose of considering your letter, we now return you this reply, and wish to say that it is the unanimous conclusion of all who have been consulted.

Your letter invites the Republicans of Utah, through their Central Committee, to take part in mass meetings, called by the People's Party "to select delegates to a convention which is to prepare a constitution, with a view to her application, by the Territory of Utah, for admission into the Union as a State." We acknowledge with pleasure, the courtesy which prompted your invitation, while we sincerely regret that the brief time permitted us for a reply, as well as for consultation, will not allow us to answer your invitation as we would desire. The exigencies of your call for the meetings to which we are invited, entitle you to an immediate reply, and we must necessarily abridge, rather than elaborate this response.

We acknowledge the importance of the sub ject of your letter. The question of State-hood for Utah involves to a great degree the most vital interests affecting the welfare and prosperity of the people of Utah, and has as we conceive, even a greater importance to the Gentile or non-Mormon portion which we represent than to those of your committee. We concede freely the gravity of the proposi-on. and shall discuss it. we hope, with the solemnity which properly attaches to it.

We regret exceedingly that your invitation by its terms assumes that the propriety and expediency of Utah becoming a State is not a question to be considered. As this is the most vital question in issue, we shall, before

concluding, discuss it, because while we cannot for other reasons, accept your invitation, we regard this question as by far the most important one belonging to the discussion.

Preliminary to that, however, we call attention to the manner in which our co-operation is sought.

You say, with a manner bordering upon the patronizing, that your committee solicit "the co-operation of the Republican party of Utah" in

YOUR MOVEMENT FOR STATEHOOD

And invite that party to take an active part in the mass conventions called by your Committee, with the assurance that if we do so we "shall be accorded a fair representation" in the proposed convention. As we are advised by the public press that a like invitation has been extended to the Democratic party of Utah, we may fairly assume that the proposition amounts to this: The People's party by its Committee having called upon its followers to elect delegates to the proposed convention which it has decided to hold, proposes that the Republicans and Democrats shall enter the People's party organization and meetings and allow such meetings to select delegates from the entire mass assembled, with the assurance that a fair representation will be "accorded" to Republicans and Democrats. Instead of our political organization choosing its own representatives from among the party, we are invited into the camp of another party, or rather two other parties, and told that these two and ourselves may select a number of Republicans, such as the whole shall decide is "fair," as delegates to the convention. Instead of the Republican party, therefore, being called upon to send delegates of its own choosing to the convention, it is asked to allow those not of its party, to select its representatives for it. Perhaps if a proposal of this kind were made by the two great national parties to each other, that is, each party should allow its opponent to select its candidates for public station, the substance of the proposition would be more readily understood; but we take it there would be no difference between such a proposition and the one submitted to us, except, that while you propose to select the Republican delegates, you do not indicate any willingness to "accord" to the Republican party, the like privilege of selecting the delegates of the People's party. Passing this, however, there is another view of the subject to which we desire to call attention. The "People's party" is admittedly a local party in Utah Territory. It claims neither connection nor affiliation with either of the great national parties of the country, and even in the situation of a candidate for the National Congress, it maintains its opposition to both those parties. It is not only a distinct party, but its followers, as is well known, are made up exclusively of one class of people in Utah—those who are adherents of the Mormon Church. This party has hitherto, as we shall show, been unsuccessful in the frequent applications it has made to secure the admission of Utah into the Union as a State, and finding this, in their opinion, a "propitious time" to renew their former efforts in that direction, desire to enlist the co-operation of those organizations which have political relations and influence, with the two great parties of the country, to aid it, in securing the success of its scheme. We are asked by the Mormon Church party, speaking plainly, not to decide upon the expediency and propriety of the measure it proposes, but to assist them to do, what they have failed to accomplish without us. In fact, your invitation while entirely polite in form, bears on its face evidence that you regard it as condescension, when you allow us—"accord" is the word—the privilege of aiding you in securing an object, about the propriety of which we have not been consulted. With all due respect we must be allowed to say, that before we give our aid to such a scheme, we should be permitted first to examine and determine upon its wisdom and propriety. Your invitation pre-determines that question, and that now is the "propitious" time for an application for admission into the Union, and without consulting us as to whether we agree with you on this vital proposition, you seem to think we should be sufficiently honored by an invitation to assist in consummating your scheme.

THE PROPOSED MOVEMENT.

This brings us naturally to the discussion of the State movement,—its object, purpose and result—its wisdom and expediency. This, in the limited time at our disposal we can only do in a very general way, leaving much unsaid which the occasion demands, and which we would not willingly omit.

Applications for the admission of Utah to the privileges and powers of a State have been repeatedly made heretofore by those who compose the "People's party" to the Congress of the United States. A constitution was framed in 1860, and an application based upon that, was made for admission as the State of Deseret. The application was refused. In 1872, another constitution was framed and again presented to Congress with a petition for admission. This was also rejected. In 1882, still another constitution was formed, and application for admission again denied. Petitions and memorials by the Legislature of Utah, under control of your party, and at public meetings called and controlled by the Mormon Church, through its political committees, have again and again urged the Congress of the United States to give Statehood to Utah. They have uniformly been disregarded, and in the discussion of other questions relating to this Territory, the sentiment in the National Congress on the question has been unmistakably adverse to the proposition. The formal attempt made in 1873 to secure the passage of that measure in Congress, was not only a failure but it was shortly after emphasized by Congressional legislation for Utah, which very clearly indicated the public sentiment of the country at that time on the subject. The calling of the constitutional convention in 1882 met with a rebuke in further special legislation by Congress for Utah. Instead, therefore, of Congress having given any indication of a desire to extend the powers of the Mormon Church, by giving over the control of Utah to it, through a State Government, it is only a few months since—whatever may be said as to the effectiveness of the legislation enacted—that Congress unmistakably indicated its purpose to restrict the powers of the organization to still narrower limits. In view of this condition of things, known to all intelligent people, we may be permitted to ask why do your committee assert that now is a "propitious" time for the renewal of the many rejected applications of Utah for admission? What change in the public sentiment of the people of the United States has taken place which justifies the assertion that now is a propitious time for your application?

WHAT CHANGE IN THE ATTITUDE

Of the People's party (the Mormon Church in political harness) on those subjects which have always presented such obstacles to Statehood has been undergone, which enables you to make such a confident announcement? If any such changes have occurred, either on the part of your party in Utah, who are anxious for recognition as a State, or on the part of the national authorities or national public sentiment, we are not advised of it. And even

— 12 —

If we were favorable to the objects of your convention, we could not with our limited information assert this to be an opportune occasion for the effort. In truth, to be frank, we suspect that in the present closely balanced condition of political parties in the United States, and in the anxiety of each to strengthen itself for future interests, your Committee have a hope that by some political alliance appealing to the necessities of one or the other of the great parties, your object, other wise hopeless, may be secured.

Your call for a convention implies, by the fact of its being made under the circumstances, that your party, and the Church organization it represents, have concluded to modify its position in some essential features.

We are free to say (and we oppose the State organization and admission on that basis) that in so far as the institution of polygamy has been an obstacle in the way of the success of the scheme of Statehood, we suppose that your organization is prepared to surrender to the public sentiment of the country, and abandon it. Any effort for admission without such a concession would be preposterous, in view of the known public sentiment throughout the country. Therefore we, in announcing our position, do so under the supposition that all objection to the admission of Utah as a State because of the attitude of those hitherto wielding her political power on the subject of polygamy, will be met by a real or seeming abandonment of this custom for the future.

OBJECTIONS NOT MET.

This question aside then, we desire to say that our objections to Utah becoming a State, are still untouched. These objections simply stated are: The masses of the people of Utah are adherents of an ecclesiastical system which forbids all harmonious relations with any system of civil government founded on the right of man to govern himself. The central idea of your system is, that all lawful government emanates by revelation from God to His priesthood, and that it is the duty of all its followers to be advised by that priesthood on all subjects of a governmental,—as well as spiritual character. Adhesion to this theory, which negatives all faithful allegiance to any authority which it does not control, has been the main cause of the hostility which the system has ever encountered among just and fair-minded people, who are not Mormons.

The Kingdom of God on earth is the Mormon Church, as its followers assert, and is destined to supplant all other governments, or rule through them. A people who believe such a doctrine cannot be entrusted with the powers of government, without the destruction of all the rights that others are guaranteed under the Republican system. A people entertaining these views are in our opinion unfit to be trusted with political power. As a matter of demonstration we know how grossly it has been abused by your people in the past, when they enjoyed it without restraint, and we see no where the slightest evidence which gives us any hope that you have in this particular "seen the error of your ways." A people who acknowledge this theocratic idea of government cannot be true and faithful citizens of any other form of civil government; they have no proper guiding principle for its administration.

If Utah shall be clothed with the forms of a State, the result would be a theocratic State in which as Mr. Cannon, one of your ablest and wisest oracles expressed it, "the voice of God would be the voice of the people" and this voice find expression through his chosen mouthpiece—the head of the Mormon Church. This political axiom of your People's party, is announced by its recognized leaders and is accepted with full faith and obedience. It reverses the entire theory upon which all Republican Governments are founded and derives the authority to govern, not from the people, but from those anointed as you claim by a divine commission to rule over them. These differences are too radical for accommodation, for our fundamental idea of all civil government is, that it is derived from the people. In a state established under a theocratic idea, a free public sentiment finds no place. It

EXTINGUISHES AND ANNIHILATES

All the fundamental beacons of the Republican government around us, and remits us to the darkness of that superstition and fanaticism which the world of intelligence and law has been struggling to escape. This element of your system, or faith, if you choose to call it such, renders it impossible for your people to live in harmony with any other community in our land. These pretensions forced your earlier leaders, almost at the dawn of your career, to leave the State of Ohio, one of the most tolerant portions of our Union, and to seek the frontier of civilization on the western boundaries of Missouri. The attempt to contemn the laws of that State, on your theory that God's people—whom you claim to be—"were a law unto themselves," soon led to that exit from the State which forms so prominent a chapter in your list of grievances against the United States government.

The same pretensions compelled you to abandon Illinois and retreat to a spot then

— 13 —

the most thoroughly isolated of any on the continent. All this occurred before those social and domestic customs, which have by the astonishment which their adoption has created, obscured the more vital objections to your system. Here, in this Paradise of the Rocky Mountains for more than ten years, your system practically unchecked and uncontrolled had full sway. What was the result? You were in open rebellion against the Government of the United States. Your prophet, then bearing the commission of Governor, as a United States officer issued his proclamation ordering the army of the Nation to depart from this Territory; your militia, called out by his order, attacked the wagon trains carrying food to troops who bore the flag of the Nation on their journey, and captured and destroyed them.

We do not refer to those incidents with a view of exciting any asperity in this discussion, but to illustrate, what we regard as the natural result of the theory of civil government, which every Mormon sanctions. Harmonious relations with any other government are impossible, because the Mormon is

EITHER A RULER OR A REBEL

If his faith is his guide. There are many incidents in the history of this Territory fully sustaining these views, but we will not recite what needs only to be alluded to to be understood.

The irregular and totally unauthorized way in which your call for this convention is issued, is itself an illustration of your crude and un-republican theory of government; without any recent discussion, even through the public press, without an enabling act of Congress, or any law of the local Legislature, or any demand from the people, your committee issues a call to its supporters, with the same apparent assurance of obedience as if your followers were sworn soldiers, marching under the orders of its commanders. Such a violation of all the usages and traditions of American government, by which the citizen is called upon to act, instead of being consulted as to whether action is advisable, only demonstrates that your call is the dictate of a church cabal which governs its own followers by the claim of "divine right," and those who do not acknowledge its authority, by the argument of power. We regard the manner of your call, its disregard of law, its violation of precedent, its unseemly and unexplained haste, as not only an insuperable objection, but as manifesting a want of capacity for civil government, and regard for the fundamental ideas

of Republican Government, which we cannot, in justice to ourselves, decline to express.

We may add to these general observations another. However we may differ otherwise you must agree with us, that in the later Congressional legislation for Utah, Congress has intended

TO LIMIT AND RESTRICT

The authority of the Church of which your committee and its followers are members. It is true that by their prominence, one or two of the practices of your people, challenging attention by their novelty as well as their importance, have received most attention; but it has not escaped you, that the way to avoid the laws of the United States, which have recently given you great concern, is to erect a jurisdiction wherein they would not operate. As this state of things has sent into exile your acknowledged head, accused of violation of the national law, and many of your leading men for like reasons, we can well understand that measures calculated to relieve such persons do not admit of any lengthy formalities being used. Like the writ of *habeas corpus*, they belong to the category of summary remedies, and are liable to betray their origin by the circumstances of their adoption. To speak in perfect sincerity, at a time and under circumstances that compel us to be respectful, and yet entirely frank, is not this sudden movement for Statehood the last resort of the leaders of your party, to free themselves from the consequences which adherence to their principles have visited upon them personally, without giving any assurance that your system, which brought them into collision with the national authority, is to be reformed? Has this movement originated in a real regard for the welfare of the people of Utah, or is it not a device to free your leaders from the unfortunate consequences of their personal defiance of the national authority? Is it to be supposed that the Gentiles, or non-Mormons if you prefer the term, as we are, would aid in that which would give a theocratic despotism to Utah, under the form of a State government, instead of that reformation of her polity, for which many of us have been laboring for long years.

Permit us to say, in conclusion, that so long as the Mormon Church shall in numbers be superior to the non-Mormon population, and shall claim and exercise

THE POWER TO CONTROL

Through its ecclesiastical authorities its members, and they recognize its authority to exact obedience to such counsel, we, as Republicans, as citizens of Utah, as American citizens, shall and will protest against any political power being exercised by them, either in a State or any other form of civil government.

Our judgment may seem to others who are not familiar with the circumstances a harsh one but you will understand our reasons when we say, that we oppose placing governmental authority in Mormon hands because we regard the system as one totally at war, with all our recognized ideas of Republican Government, and incapable of being so reformed, as to be made in any degree a depository of impartial governing power.

When your Mormon church shall have abanponed its pretensions as a temporal power, when its people shall render that obedience to the laws of the land which is yielded by all other citizens, of every shade of religious belief, in fine, become supporters of the lawful civil government, then we will consider whether Utah, though Mormon in population,

may not be safely trusted with Statehood. Certainly for the present we cannot consent to make the experiment.

Regretting again that our differences are too radical to admit of co-operation, and hoping that the time may come when we shall recognize a common allegiance to the Government of our country, and that each man's faith in religion, may be such as to harmonize with his duty as a citizen, we are most respectfully

Your obedient servants,

WM. F. JAMES, Chairman.

WILLIAM NELSON, Secretary.

M. M. KAIGHN,
JOHN R. MCBRIDE,
ARTHUR BROWN,
P. H. EMERSON,
E. P. FERRY,
JOS. E GALIGHER
V. M. C. SILVA,
CHRIS DIEHL,

Members Territorial Republican Committee.

VOICE OF THE NON-MORMONS.

The non-Mormons of Utah, in Liberal Convention assembled, July 20th, 1887, adopted the following resolutions :

Resolv d, FIRST: That, so long as the temporal power of the Mormon Church shall remain in issue, and as long as that church, as a political organizatl)n, continues to array itself against the laws of the land, a sense of self-preservation as well as true allegiance to the Republic and its free institutions, calls on all true American citizens in the Territory to stand and act together against a great overshadowing evil as they do now, without differences as to national politics: and we, therefore, affirm it to be the duty and purpose of all such, to support the Liberal organization, as a broad, common ground, adapted to the necessities of the situation, from which we can best appeal to both National parties in Congress and the sense of the Nation at large.

SECOND: That the dominant majority in Utah, having persistently disregarded and opposed the laws of the land, by prostituting the powers of a Territorial government and otherwise, cannot safely be trusted with the powers of a State government.

THIRD: That the proposed State Constitution is a device of the Mormon Church to enable its priesthood to perpetuat :, by State control, their harsh temporal power and corrupt social system which has blighted Utah for the last thirty-five years.

FOURTH: That, in our opinion, based on a thorough acquaintance with the political methods of the Mormon Church, the provisions of the constitution, concocted and proposed by its agents, prohibiting certain crimes heretofore inculcated as part of its creed, enjoined by divine revelation, are deceitful and false, and are a mere paltering in a double sense, contrived to mislead a generous and forgiving Nation, and to secure a continued lease of power: being heretofore and still arrayed as a unit against the execution of existing National laws to the same purport (which has been the sole ground for loud complaints of perse_cution,) no one could expect them to execute these provisions against themselves, because all experience proves that constitutions and laws which are not founded on public opinion and approved by those who administer them, can never have any force or vitality.

FIFTH: That to commit to Mormon hands the power to govern Utah as a State, with past experience of the treasonable and un-Ameri can character of that organization, would be to abandon all faithful American citizens who reside here, with all their material interests, to the oppression and misrule of a power that has never been faithful to any patriotic duty, or obedient to any law which prohibits its crimes.

SIXTH: That the perversion of delegated political power and the pernicious teachings of the politico-religious organization in Utah, for a generation, have led the dominant majority astray from all true conceptions of free government, and unfited them for the duties and responsibilities of self-government.

SEVENTH: That, until convalescence shall come to the sick body, politic and social, which has been gathered and organized politically in Utah, in blasphemous travesty as "the Kingdom of God," and until time shall have proven that the "deep damnation" of its infection has been eradicated, considerations for the public p·ace and National honor alike demand that Utah should be kept in quarantine.

EIGHTH: That the present movement for Statehood for Utah, like its seveal predecesors, having been initiated by the Mormon Church, and carried forward solely by its mem bers and agents, for its sinister purposes, and without authority or form of law, it is the sense of this convention that no American citizen in Utah who is not a member of the Mormon organization should vote at the ensuing election, either for or against the proposed constitution, or in any manner recognize the movement, except by an earnest appeal to Congress and the Nation to save us from the great calamity thus threatened. At the same time, we earnestly urge all Liberals in the Territory to support their respective legislative and county tickets.

NINTH: That the Utah Commission owes its existence to the fact recognized by repeated acts of Congress that the dominant majority of Utah are unfit to be invested with the usual powers of a Territorial government; that the hasty action of a majority of that Commission in attempting to lend their official sanction to the movement for Statehood under control of a disloyal majority, is a stultification of their previous action in like cases, a usurpation of power without any color of law, and presents the painful spectacle of impotent spectators, without power to do any effective good in Utah, lending their official influence to promote and perpetuate the evils which their employment was intended to repress and extinguish.

TENTH: That we protest against the action of the manager of the Associated Press dispatches in taking from the regular agent the business of framing the dispatches from Utah during the progress of the late convention, and committing that business exclusively to the Mormon organization, as a prostitution of that powerful agency, and a part of an existing conspiracy to procure Statehood for them by false representations, and we warn the public everywhere against those mendacious fabrications.

ELEVENTH: That a committee of five be appointed by the chair to draft an address to the President, Congress and the country, protesting against the admission of Utah as a State under existing conditions, and that copies thereof be forwarded to them and to the press of the country.

REPORT

OF THE

UTAH COMMISSION

TO THE

SECRETARY OF THE INTERIOR,

FOR THE YEAR 1887.

SALT LAKE CITY:
TRIBUNE PRINT.

1887.

REPORT.

SIR: The great interest which has been manifested by Congress and the people generally in the affairs of Utah Territory, has led us to believe that the following statements with respect to the Territory and its citizens will prove to be interesting information, especially so in view of recent events which have transpired in the Territory.

AREA.

Utah Territory has a maximum length of 325 miles by a breadth of 300. Its land area is 84,970 square miles (52,601,600 acres) water area, 2780 square miles, (1,779,200 acres.) Nearly 13,000,000 acres of land have been or are now in progress of survey. Up to July 1, 1887, nearly 4,500,000 acres had been disposed of by the Government. Area.

STATEMENT

Showing the valuation of property assessed in the several counties of the Territory of Utah; also, the amount of property assessed in the name of non-Mormons, Railroads, Western Union Telegraph and Telephone Companies for the year 1886. (Mines not included.)

COUNTIES.	Total Valuation.	Am't Belonging to Non-Mormons.	Am't Assessed to R R's., W. U. Tel. and Tel'n Cos
Beaver	$ 771,805	$ 181,558	$ 103,702
Box Elder	2,209,425	160,805	1,379,971
Cache	2,075,460	232,684	117,358
Davis	1,124,713	74,314	235,473
Emery	825,011	224,050	425,380
Garfield	173,807	25,375	
Iron	434,415	14,454	
Juab	1,078,751	85,151	299,606
Kane	206,518	26,570	
Millard	867,863	151,575	364,073
Morgan	397,626	34,834	185,589
Piute	219,888	48,125	
Rich	350,170	113,894	
Salt Lake	12,457,625	4,690,790	526,795
San Juan	304,760	*160,000	
Sanpete	1,257,333	173,072	18,956
Sevier	550,743	*159,025	
Summit	1,725,080	*760,000	407,000
Tooele	1,012,761	107,216	109,420
Uintah	139,825	91,056	
Utah	3,240,676	506,162	528,475
Wasatch	356,658	62,500	
Washington	726,151	71,783	
Weber	3,158,738	976,466	405,216
*Estimated. Total	$35,665,802	$9,131,459	$5,107,014

Valuation of property.

EXPLANATORY NOTE.—In Summit county the estimate was made upon the information received from a member of the County Court. In Sevier and San Juan counties upon information received from reliable sources.

The non-Mormons own within a fraction of 25.61
per cent; the Mormons own 60.07 per cent, assuming
that all the remaining property, excepting railroads,
etc., belongs to them. This, however, is not the fact,
as there is a considerable amount of property belonging
to non-Mormons in the different counties which could
not be identified as to ownership. The railroads, etc.,
represent within a fraction of 14.32 per cent. They are
owned by non-Mormons excepting a minority interest
in the Utah Central and one other small road.

Percentage of property owned by Mormons and non-Mormons.

POPULATION.

The first census of the Territory of Utah, taken in
1850, showed the population to be 11,380; the census of
1860, 40,273; of 1870, 86,786, and the latest, that of 1880,
143,963. The gain from 1850 to 1860 was 28,893, or 250
per cent; from 1860 to 1870, 46,513, 110 per cent, or 1150
for every 1000 of population; from 1870 to 1880, 66 per
cent, or 660 for every 1000. The total gain from 1870
to 1880 was 23 per cent greater than the total increase
from 1860 to 1870. If the same relative gain has continued from 1880 to 1887, the increase would be 22 per
cent greater than from 1870 to 1880, and 43 per cent
greater than from 1860 to 1870, or a population in 1887
of 210,478. We estimate, however, the population at
200,000.

Population.

The prosperity of the past seven years has been
equal to that of any former period of the history of the
Territory. The leading cities and towns, and many of
the smaller communities, show a steady and gratifying
growth. In the more remote counties the settlements
have been gradually creeping to places formerly the
habitat of wild animals, and the hunting ground of
the Indian, supposed to be too desolate for habitation.
Emery county, which had but two organized precincts
in 1880, has twelve in 1887; Piute county, four in 1880,
eleven in 1887, etc.

General prosperity.

There is every reason to claim that the same relative gain has been maintained, and that Utah now has a population of at least 200,000. This population is divided into two elements—Mormon and non-Mormon.

THE MORMON ELEMENT.

The Mormon element consists of the members of the Church of Jesus Christ of Latter-Day Saints.

On April 1st, 1887, the total Mormon population in the Territories of Utah, Idaho, Arizona, Wyoming and New Mexico, and the States of Nevada and Colorado was 162,383, officially classed and ranked as follows: 3 first presidents, 11 apostles, 65 patriarchs, 6444 seventies, 3723 high priests, 12,441 elders. 2423 priests, 2497 teachers, 6854 deacons, and 81,283 members; total officers and members, 115,699. Children under eight years of age, 46,684. Grand total of souls, 162,383.

Mormon population in Utah, Idaho, Arizona, etc.

In the Territory of Utah the total number of officers and members and children under eight years of age was 132,297. (Children are baptized at the age of eight, and received as members.)

The first Mormon settlement in the great intermountain basin was made at Salt Lake City, July 24th, 1847. From thence the settlements have gradually extended along the base of the mountains wherever water could be found to irrigate the soil, until now they reach from as far north as the shores of the Bear Lake, Idaho, to the banks of the Gila, Arizona, on the south, and from the western part of Colorado, Wyoming and New Mexico, to Southeastern Nevada. These settlements with but few exceptions have been made in the agricultural belt. At first the settlers experienced many of the hardships incident to pioneer life, but they met them cheerfully, and were delighted with the prospect before them.

Mormon settlements, where located.

They had come to "a glorious valley to locate and build up Zion," and, as they believed, where they could

practice undisturbed by human laws the peculiar teachings of their religious faith. They found a fertile soil,
formed by denundations from the mountains which had
Character of the soil and climate. always, from the day it was first disturbed by the plow-
share, been profusely bountiful in its yield, and the
declivities of the mountains covered with bunch grass
(wild wheat) which furnished rich pasturage to their
cattle. They also found a climate not surpassed by that
of any portion of the country where the rays of the
summer sun are tempered by the cool breezes from the
cañons, and the severity of the winter is softened by the
mountains which shelter the valleys. These beautiful
valleys are now dotted with thriving settlements and
have the appearance of a vast garden watered from an
infinite number of irrigating canals, the result of the
industry of the people.

The settlements have been organized into bishops'
Number of bis-hops' wards. wards, and the wards into stakes of Zion. The boundaries of the wards are mainly coextensive with the pre-
cinct lines, and the boundaries of the stakes with the
county lines. There are in Utah 293 wards,
in Idaho 52, in Arizona 29, in Nevada 6, in
Colorado 4, in Wyoming 3, and in New Mexico 2,
a total of 389. There are in Utah, 18 stakes, in Arizona
Number of stakes. 3, in Idaho 2, in Colorado 1, and 6 partly in Utah and
some one of the surrounding States and Territories.
The wards are presided over by a bishop, two counselors,
and a corps of officers, priests, teachers and deacons,
The presiding officers of the wards, stakes and church. who look after the different districts into which the
wards are divided. The stakes are presided over by a
president and two counselors, with a similar corps of
officers to assist them. The entire church is presided
over by either a First Presidency or an Apostles' quorum. Three times in the history of the church a First
Presidency has been organized, the last, consisting of
John Taylor with George Q. Cannon and Joseph F.
Smith as his Counselors. The death of John Taylor has

dissolved the First Presidency, and the government of the church now rests upon the quorum of the Twelve Apostles, of which Wilford Woodruff, an aged and ener- The present head getic man is president. He is now the virtual head of Church. of the Mormon the church, which will continue to be governed by the Apostles, it is presumed, until another revelation is received reviving the First Presidency.

The wards report to the stakes, the stakes to the head of the church. There are, however, other officers Organizations in and organizations of importance in the church. There Church. the Mormon are seven first presidents of the seventies. The seven-ties are local organizations, consisting of a quorum of seventy elders. Each of these organizations is governed by seven presidents, and each of the seven presidents by a president. There is a presiding bishop of the church, whose most important duty seems to be the col-lection of the tithes (he has agents, one in each of the stakes), and a head patrjarch who blesses the people by the laying on of hands. There is also a high council in each of the stakes whose work is done in secret. In each of the ward districts the quorum of teachers are directed to visit each family periodically and look after their spiritual welfare. Each ward has a meeting house, Young Men's Mutual Improvement Society, Primary Association for young children and a Relief Society.

The various organizations report semi-annually, and there is kept at the church office in Salt Lake City, a Statistical complete statistical history of the church. The number history. of members, marriages, births, deaths, baptisms, excom-munications, etc., are set forth in detail.

The Mormons believe in the Bible (Old and New Testament), the Book of Mormon, and the revelations Religious belief. claimed to have been made to the prophets of the church. These revelations relate to various subjects, from the apportionment of town property down to the naming of church officers and affairs connected with the church government. One of the revelations known as the "Word of Wisdom," counsels the people not to use strong drinks, tobacco and hot drinks (tea and coffee).

Revelation commanding polygamy. The revelation commanding polygamy was said to have been received from the Lord by Joseph Smith in Nauvoo, Hancock county, Illinois, July 12, 1843. Its binding force upon the Mormon people, believing as they do in their church and its teaching, will be understood from the following extract:

"For behold! I reveal unto you a new and everlasting covenant; and if ye abide not that covenant, then are ye damned, for no one can reject this covenant, and be permitted to enter my glory."

Obedience exacted from members. In the church government obedience is exacted from every member. In removing from one ward to another, they must secure a recommendation from their bishop, which certifies to their standing in the church. Persons desiring to be married, or to enter into polygamy, must also secure a recommendation from the bishop of their ward. Every member must hold himself ready, irrespective of personal considerations, to leave his home to go as a missionary to other lands, and he must also be ready to remove his family and effects to such place as the heads of the church may direct him to go. The Mormon settlements in Arizona and other places outside Utah, were made in obedience to such a command. At the Utah stake conference held Feb. 27th, 1881, the names of 29 heads of families were announced as missionaries for permanent settlement at St. Johns, Arizona. In a few weeks these families were on their way to make a new home in a strange place. At other conferences held in Southern stakes, at different times, many families were sent as missionaries to Arizona.

Mormon Church courts. The Mormon Church teaches its members not to enter the Territorial courts to settle their difficulties. It has provided a system of courts within the church. First, there is a ward court known or designated as a "bishop's court," consisting of the bishop and his two Their authority and power. counselors. They are empowered to try all minor cases arising among the people both of a temporal and of a

spiritual nature, and to sit in judgment upon trans-
gressors.

For a long period they assumed jurisdiction of questions of martial separation and divorce, but we are not
advised as to whether this jurisdiction is still exercised.
From this court an appeal lies to the "Stake Court," ^{Same.}
consisting of the president of the stake and his two
counselors. This court has also original jurisdiction.
The court of last resort, possessing appellate, original
and exclusive jurisdiction, is the First Presidency, or the
Apostles' Quorum, as the case may be. The mandate of
this court must be accepted and obeyed, under penalty
of excommunication, which means a denial of all the
benefits of the church, social ostracism, and a with-
drawal of the patronage and support of the Mormon
people.

The payment of tithing and other donations for the
support of the church is vigorously urged as a religious ^{Tithing, amount of.}
duty. At a church conference, President John Taylor
said:

"You want to pay your tithing honestly and squarely, or you will find
yourselves outside the pale of the church of the living God."

The amounts collected from the people for tithing
exceed $500,000 annually. In 1870, the amount was
$425,000; in 1880, $540,000. The amounts received for
temple building are also very large. At the October ^{Cost of temples.}
conference of 1880, it was announced that the uncom-
pleted Manti and Logan temples had cost to date, re-
spectively $207,977.35 and $252,147.78. The building of
the Salt Lake Temple was commenced September 6th,
1853, and will not be finished for years to come. It has
cost millions of dollars. The church has become quite
wealthy. In 1880, John Taylor stated that the church ^{Wealth of the Mormon Church.}
held $430,000 of the paid-up capital stock of Zion's
Co-operative Mercantile Institution, which pays large
dividends, and which was organized by Brigham Young
for the purpose of depriving non-Mormons of Mormon

patronage. It owns or did own, the Deseret Telegraph system; the Zion's Savings Bank; the *Deseret Evening News;* the Deseret paper mill; a church farm south of Salt Lake City of over 1300 acres; street railway stock; stock in the Deseret and other National Banks; railroad shares and bonds; and a large amount of real estate in Salt Lake City and elsewhere, of great value.

The heads of the church teach and impress upon the people to be united and submissive in their political action to the will of the leaders of the church. At a general conference of the church, President Taylor said:

Control of political action by Mormon Church.

"We have to lay aside our covetousness and our pride, and our ideas that are wrong, and be united in our political affairs, in our temporal affairs, under the direction of the holy priesthood, and act as a mighty phalanx under God in carrying out his purposes here upon this earth."

In connection with this exercise of political control is the dream of empire which all through their history has cheered them with its pleasing illusions of future power. They teach and preach, and apparently believe, that the portion of the country in which they now reside was set apart to become the abiding place of the Saints, where is to be erected the kingdom of God upon earth. Their missionaries preach that God has commanded his people to gather to the mountains, to the Zion of the Lord, to receive their inheritance at the hands of his servants. This idea is very clearly set forth by Brigham Young in a remarkable thanksgiving proclamation from him as Governor of the Territory, dated December 19th, 1851. We reproduce the opening paragraph. The italics are ours:

Political empire.

"It having pleased the Father of all good, to make known his mind and will to the children of men, in these last days, and through the ministration of His angels, to restore the Holy Priesthood unto the sons of Adam, by which the Gospel of His son has been proclaimed, and the ordinances of life and salvation are administered, and through which medium the Holy Ghost has been communicated to believing, willing and honest minds; causing faith, wisdom and intelligence to spring up in the hearts of men, and influencing them to flow together from the four quarters of the earth to a land of peace and health, rich in mineral and vegetable resources, *reserved of old in the Councils of eternity for the purposes to which it is now appropriated;* a land of choice above all other lands, far removed from strife, contention, divisions, moral and physical commotions, that are disturbing the peace of the nations and kingdoms of the earth."

The church leaders have been very much disturbed by the sale of property to non-Mormons, and have from the pulpit urged upon the people not to sell their inheritance in Zion, that has been entrusted to them to carry out the purposes of the Lord, and not for purposes of gain.

The people are very tenacious of what they claim to be their rights, *and have never yielded a point.* They stand to-day where they stood when they first entered the Territory. They persistently claim that they have been persecuted. September 29th, 1851, in a letter to the President, Governor Young said:

Mormons have never yielded a point.

"That no people exist who are more friendly to the Government of the United States, than the people of this Territory. The Constitution they revere, the laws they seek to honor. But the non-execution of those laws in times past for our protection, and the abuse of the power in the hands of those we have supported for office, even betraying us in the hour of our greatest peril and extremity, by withholding the due execution of the laws designed for the protection of all the citizens of the United States."

Protestations of loyalty.

Similar protestations of loyalty have been made from time to time down to a very recent period.

Undoubtedly in Missouri and Illinois, they were the victims of many unlawful attacks; but there has always been something in their methods which has excited the opposition and the distrust of every people among whom they have lived. They have been invited and had it in their power while in Utah, to settle honorably the contest which has been waged between the Government and them. All that has been asked of them is to acknowledge the supremacy of the law.

Distrust of their methods.

What has been asked of them by the Government.

The Mormons control a Territory almost as large as the area of the States of New York and Pennsylvania combined, and a controlling influence in a tract of territory as large as that of the New England and Middle

Area of territory controlled by the Mormon Church.

States combined. They have established in this Territory a religious system, with a political attachment, the two forming a strong, compact government with the power of control centered in a few men who claim the right to speak by divine right, and whose advice, counsel and command is a law unto the people.

Characteristics of the people.

The majority of the Mormons are a kindly and hospitable people. They possess many traits of character which are well worthy of emulation by others. In their local affairs they strive to suppress the vices which are common to settled communities. In matters of religion they are intensely devotional, rendering a cheerful obedience to their church rules and requirements. They are a people who possess many of the elements, which, under wise leadership, would make them useful and prosperous.

NON-MORMON ELEMENT.

Strength of the non-Mormon element.

The strength of the non-Mormon element cannot be accurately stated. The population of the Territory has been given at 200,000. If from this be deducted the strength of the Mormon element, 132,277, we have 67,723 not claimed by the Mormon Church, but of these there are many whose sympathies remain with it. They have been raised in Mormonism, and although they have drifted away, they probably act with their former friends in political matters. The non-Mormon strength will probably not exceed 55,000.

Their work in the mines.

In Salt Lake City and Ogden they have prosperous communities, mainly engaged in business. The strength of the element, however, is to be found in the mining camps. Gold and silver mining began in Utah in 1869-70. Since then a vast amount of capital has been invested in the mines. The great body of the Gentiles are equal in intellect, courage and energy to those of any other community. When they went to Utah they found all the agricultural land that had water conveni-

ent already appropriated. Both the land and the water
had been secured, and land without water is practically
worthless for agriculture in that Territory. There was
nothing left for them but the mines. These they
searched for and as found, opened. This is work that
none but superior men can carry through. It takes capital, courage, faith, sagacity, endurance and ceaseless
work. Of all the mines found, some have brought rich
returns. But of these a vast proportion goes for labor,
for supplies, for machinery and to make roads. Silver
mines are generally found among almost inaccessible
mountain tops, and every movement connected with
them is costly. These mines have yielded up to the
present time, $96,000,000. Quite half the sum has been Yield of the mines.
paid to Mormons for labor and supplies, and through
this from a very poor people they have become very
prosperous. They possessed the land when the Gentiles
went among them, but they were so poor that some
whole families did not secure $10 in money throughout
the year. What the Gentiles have been able to accomplish has been in spite of the Mormon combined compe-
tition and opposition. They wrenched from the rugged
and barren mountain tops the gold and silver until they
own of the assessed property of the Territory, nearly
one-third, exclusive of railroad property.

A brief description of the Little Cottonwood Dis-
trict, where mining is conducted under more than ordi- Little Cotton-
nary difficult circumstances will convey an adequate wood Mining District.
idea of the toil and danger which attends, and of the
superior abilities required for successful mining. This
mining district is located in Little Cottonwood Cañon,
the mouth of which is some 15 miles distant from Salt
Lake City. Entering the cañon the granite walls rise
4000 feet above the valley. The granite forms the cone
around which the mountains have grown until their
peaks are 13,000 feet above the level of the sea, and
nearly 8000 feet above the valley. Passing up the cañon

the granite walls continue for five miles, rising in grandeur far above the tramway which transports passengers and freight to the mining town of Alta, eight miles above. The grade is over 350 feet to the mile. Snow sheds cover the rails nearly the whole distance. Leaving the granite we pass a great quartzite reef, interspersed with shales. Above this the limestones (the silurian, devonian and carboniferous) rise in succession. In the limestones the ore is found, and scattered around the steep declivities can be seen the cabins of the miners. The rock is so hard that the average cost of tunneling is some $10.00 per foot. Miles of tunnels have been run at an enormous cost. The snow commences to fall in August and September and continues until the following May. The average fall is 30 feet. At Alta City, where the elevation is nearly 9000 feet, the average depth covering the ground the winter through is 15 feet. The citizens communicate with each other through tunnels run under the snow. The tramway is closed in the early fall, and the only means of communication with the valley below for six months of the year is by a hazardous trip down the cañon through the deep snow. The snow gathers around the summits of the peaks in such heavy masses that snow slides are of frequent occurrence. Since 1870, 132 persons have perished in this cañon from these slides, and the town of Alta has been repeatedly swept as if by a cyclone. Many of the miners work in the mines all the year round. One has built a cabin under the summit of "Old Baldy," a peak between the Little Cottonwood and American Fork cañons, 10,-500 feet above the level of the sea. In these altitudes the rocks, which lift their heads through the soil, become bare. The tempests have left them naked and gray. A life in these vast solitudes is not very enchanting, and yet thousands of energetic, able and patriotic men pass their lives among them, the great majority deprived of many of the comforts of life, and by unremitting toil contributing to the material wealth of the Territory.

Leaving the mining camps and returning to the valleys, we find the non-Mormons supplying the majority of the capital which is invested in the different avenues of business, and the brains which give life and force to the different channels of trade. They are also engaged in the important work of educating the youth of the Territory. By their efforts mission schools have been established in Salt Lake City, Ogden, and nearly every community of importance in the Territory, which have been very successful. In Salt Lake City the Protestant Episcopal Church established its first school in 1867. Then it had a school with 16 pupils; now it has four schools, 29 teachers and 589 pupils. The Methodist Church opened its first school September 20th, 1870, with 28 pupils; now they have 20 schools with 36 teachers and 1060 pupils. The Presbyterians opened their first school April 12, 1875, with 30 pupils; now they have 33 schools with 67 teachers and 2110 pupils. The Salt Lake Academy opened its doors in the fall of 1878, under the auspices of the Congregational Church. They had in 1886, 22 schools with 43 teachers and 1900 pupils. The Baptist Church came into the Territory in 1884. They have one school with one teacher and 74 scholars. The first Catholic school was commenced in the fall of 1875; they now have 6 schools with 53 teachers and 880 pupils. The Swedish Lutheran Church opened a school last year with one teacher and 35 pupils. A grand total of 87 schools, 230 teachers and 6668 scholars.

These different denominations have now in Utah 62 churches of the value of $453,950 as follows:

	No. of Churches.	Value.
Protestant Episcopal	4	$127,650
Methodist	26	119,000
Catholic	6	25,300
Presbyterian	18	115,000
Congregational	*5	25,000
Swedish Lutheran	1	12,000
Baptist	1	25,000
Josephite Mormon	1	5,000

*Also, 12 preaching stations.

Work of the non-Mormons.

Schools established.

Churches.

The non-Mormons have always been regarded as
intruders in Utah, and are referred to as "outsiders."
Within the past five years one of the First Presidency
of the Mormon Church in an address delivered in the
Mormon Tabernacle, in sustance said, "We ought never
to have let them secure a foothold here." And this
expresses the sentiments of the great majority of the
Mormon people. They attribute the troubles which
have come to their leaders, to the presence of these
"outsiders," and not to the awakened public sentiment
of the Nation. The non-Mormons, who have played a
conspicuous part in the work of reforming the Territory,
are referred to as "aggressive persons," "blatant assail-
ants of the religion and politics of the majority of the
business men and people of the Territory." "Conspira-
tors" and "adventurers." In illustration of this feeling
we refer to the organization of the Chamber of Commerce at Salt Lake City. This movement was made
under the lead of Governor West, and business men of
every shade of opinion were invited to participate and
to work for the common benefit of all. The prominent
non-Mormons became members of the Chamber. The
Deseret Evening News, the authorized exponent of the
views of the Mormon church, speaking of the movement
and referring to them, said:

How non-Mormons are regarded by the Mor-
mons.

"How much harmony can be expected in such a heterogeneous com-
mingling of antagonistic forces? If the business men of the Territory
want to work together for business purposes, all such plotters against the
peace of the Territory and obsacles to its material interests will necessarily
have to withdraw or be removed from the organization. How can any man
with self-respect fraternize and hold intimate relations with persons who
have deliberately plotted and labored with all their might to misrepresent
him and his friends and rob them of every political right that is valued by
free men? Through their efforts the wives, daughters, sisters and mothers
of the business men who are invited to help boom these agitators into
influence and prosperity have been deprived of the franchise and relegated
to political serfdom, on a level with felons, idiots and lunatics."

This extract thoroughly explains the feeling entertained by the majority against those of the minority

who have been persistent in urging Congress to provide
a remedy for the evils which they believe to exist here.
The Chamber of Commerce was organized, is prosperous,
and ha⁼ proved a valuable ally to the business community.

The non-Mormon element has brought to Utah, Work accomplished by the
enterprise and capital, the school-book and the Bible. non-Mormons.
Their mining industries have created a market for the
sale of the surplus products of the Mormon farmer, and
employment for the surplus labor; their schools and
churches are promoting the temporal and spiritual
welfare of the people.

The majority of the non-Mormons impress us as
being enterprising and public spirited citizens who are
warmly attached to their county and its laws.

THE POLITICAL HISTORY OF UTAH AND POLYGAMY.

The political history of the Territory of Utah and
the system of plural marriage are so closely interwoven Political history
of the Territory
that the one cannot be considered separate and apart from and polygamy.
the other. In fact, since July 24,1847, polygamy has given
tone to the political policy of the Mormon people. Under
the provisional government of the State of Deseret, and the
Territorial government which followed after, every act
of the Legislative Assembly which had, even remotely,
a political bearing was voted up or down solely
upon the question of its relation to the overshadowing interest. Every effort has been made to
strengthen polygamy which the experience of 40 years
could suggest, and every chord has been struck which
it was supposed might send back a responsive and
friendly note.

The result has been that nearly every man of prom-
inence in the church became a polygamist; the control- Control of the
Territory by
ling intellect of Utah became involved in the practice. polygamists.
They filled nearly every office of importance in the
church, and in the Territorial and county governments,
and had a large majority of every Legislative Assembly

down to the year 1882, when the "Edmunds Law" dis qualified them. Utah was governed by men who seemed determined to build up in the heart of the American continent a polygamous empire.

The statistics for 1880 will give an idea of how far they had progressed.

The strength of the polygamous class.

The census found a population of 143,962, of which 60,576 were over 21 years of age; about 10,000 of these are estimated to be non-Mormons. The number of persons then living in polygamy was found, after careful inquiry, to be about 12,000, and there were at least 3000 who had lived in polygamy, but a separation had been effected by death or otherwise, making a total of 15,000, 30 per cent of the adult Mormon population, or one out of every 3 1-3 who had entered into polygamy. While all did not enter into polygamy, all believed it right as a divine revelation and upheld it in those who chose to enter into the relation. The system was united by ties of kindred with nearly every Mormon family in the Territory.

The government of Utah before the organization of the Territory.

Utah was controlled by the bishops of the church, under the direction of Brigham Young, from July 24, 1847, to March 18, 1849, at which time was organized the provisional government of the State of Deseret. The Apostles of the Church in a general epistle said they had petitioned Congress for the organization of a Territorial government, and, until the petition was granted, they were under the necessity of organizing a local government. Brigham Young was elected Governor of the State. The most important act of the Legislative Assembly of the new State was the incorporation of the Church of Jesus Christ of Latter-day Saints.

Incorporation of the Mormon Church.

Section 3, which we here reproduce, under the form of law, we think, directly sanctioned the practice of polygamy.

"SEC. 3. And be it further ordained: That, as said Church holds the Constitutional and original right, in common with all civil and religious communities, "to worship God according to the dictates of conscience;" to reverence communion agreeably to the principles of truth, and to solemnize marriage compatible with the revelations of Jesus Christ; for the security and full enjoyment of all blessings and privileges, embodied in the religion of Jesus Christ, free to all; it is also declared that said church does, and shall possess and enjoy continually, the power and authority, in and of itself, to originate, make, pass and establish rules, regulations, ordinances, laws, customs and criterions, for the good order, safety, government, conveniences, comfort, and control of said church; and for the punishment and forgiveness of all offenses, relative to fellowship, according to church covenants; that the pursuit of bliss; and the enjoyment of life, in the capacity of public association and domestic happiness, temporal expansion, or spiritual increase upon the earth, may not legally be questioned. Provided, however, that each and every act, or practice so established, or adopted for law, or custom, shall relate to solemnities, sacraments, ceremonies, consecrations, endowments, tithings, marriages, fellowship, or the religious duties of man to his Maker; inasmuch as the doctrines, principles, practices, or performances, support virtue, and increase morality. and are not inconsistent with, or repugnant to, the Constitution of the United States, or of this State, and are founded in the revelations of the Lord."

The Edmunds-Tucker act of March, 1887, annulled this act, and directed the Attorney-General of the United States to close up the affairs of the church. *Incorporation act annulled.*

Jan. 27, 1851, the news reached Salt Lake City that Congress had created the Territory of Utah, and that President Fillmore had appointed Brigham Young Territorial Governor. No appointment could have been made which would have been more satisfactory to the Mormons. Brigham Young was their leader, ruler and prophet. He was re-appointed Governor by President Pierce, and served till July 11, 1857. The influence of this appointment upon the future of Utah was far-reaching. It enabled the Mormon people to adopt a system of laws which gave them absolute control over the Territorial government, and stripped the Federal officers of all authority and power. At an early day laws were passed conferring upon Probate Courts, concurrent jurisdiction with the District Courts and, owing to the claim and exercise of jurisdiction by these Probate Courts under Territorial laws, the District Courts as representatives of the *Organization of the Territory. Appointment of Brigham Young as Governor. Results which followed the appointment. Federal officers deprived of all power.*

National authority, continued to be practically nullities
until 1874. In 1874 (by the Poland Act) Congress defined
and limited the jurisdiction of the several grades of
courts in the Territory.

The act as it passed the House of Representatives
placed the power of naming jurors for the Courts with
the U. S. Marshal; but by a provision of the Act imposed
at its last stage, the power to name one-half of the
panel was restored to the old agency: by reason of
which, acts of Congress distasteful to Utah, remained
dead letters till 1882-3 when the "Edmunds Act" disqualified Mormons from jury service in polygamy and
unlawful cohabitation cases. In 1885 it was held and
affirmed in the case of Rudger Clawson, indicted for
polygamy, that the District Courts were not confined to
the panel so named, but after its exhaustion might resort to an open venire. This decision removed the clog
from the enforcemeut of the laws which had existed
over 30 years (the result which followed from the appointment of Brigham Yonng as Governor); prosecutions
and convictions for polygamy and unlawful cohabitation
under the laws of Congress became possible and so successful and efficient have these prosecutions been for
three years past that a great number of convictions,
particularly for the latter offence, have been had, and a
large number of offenders, including the most prominent and influential leaders, have fled or gone into concealment, to avoid conviction. In furtherance of the
purpose of obtaining control of the Territory, an independent military organization was established by law
in violation of the organic act which makes the Governor of the Territory "Commander-in-chief of the militia
thereof." This independent organization was forced to
disband by Gov. Shaffer in 1870.

Laws were also adopted for the election of certain officers which the organic act imposes upon

Provision of the "Poland" Act and "Edmunds" Act with reference to jurors.

Jurors selected by open venire.

Effect of the prosecutions for polygamy and unlawful cohabitation.

Independent military organization created.

the Governor the duty of appointing. The At-torney-General of the United States has decided the power to appoint lies with the Governor; but the Legislative Assembly presistently refuses to remedy the wrong.

In 1851, polygamy was publicly proclaimed as a tenet of the church by alleged "Divine revelation," by Brigham Young, President of the Mormon Church, and Governor of the Territory.

At a special Conference of the Mormon Church, held at Salt Lake City during the same year, was begun the controversy between the Mormon people and the representatives of the Federal Government which has continued to the present time. Judge Brocchus of the Territorial Supreme Court, who was present, rebuked the people for their polygamous practices. His speech was, as he said, "the result of deliberation and care." It gave great offence to Brigham Young and the Mormon people, who charged him with falsifying "the eternal principles of truth," and with insulting the Mormon women.

From 1851 to 1862, polygamy flourished unchecked and uncontrolled. The Mormon people claim that plural marriage during this period was not unlawful. Certainly there was no statute law against the practice of polygamy, and if the common law did not come into the Territory at the time the United States acquired possession, they are right; but it is an indisputable fact that the common law was in full force during these years. The act of 1862 provides that "every person having a husband or wife living, who marries another, whether married or single, in a Territory or other place, over which the United States has exclusive jurisdiction, is guilty of polygamy, and shall be punished by a fine of not more than $500, and by imprisonment for a term of not more than five years." The Mormon people claimed the law was not constitutional. At the first

session of the Legislative Assembly following, Governor
Harding in his message said:

"I respectfully call your attention to an act of Congress passed the
first day of July 1862, entitled 'An Act to punish and prevent the practice
of polygamy in the Territories of the United States and in other places,
and disapproving and anulling certain acts of the Territorial Legislative
Assembly of the Territory of Utah.' I am aware that there is a prevailing
opinion here that said act is unconstitutional, and therefore it is recommended by those in high authority that no regard be paid to the same;
and, still more to be regretted, if I am rightly informed, in some instances it
has been recommended that it be openly disregarded and *defied*, merely to
defy the same. I take this occasion to warn the people of this Territory
against such dangerous and disloyal courses. Whether such act is unconstitutional or not is not necessary for me either to affirm or deny. The
individual citizen, under no circumstances whatever, has the right to defy
any law or statute of the United States with impunity. In so doing he
takes upon himself the risk of the penalties of that statute, be they what
they may, in case his judgment be in error. The Constitution has amply
provided how and where all such questions of doubt are to be submitted
and settled, viz., in the courts constituted for that purpose. To forcibly
resist the execution of that act would be, to say the least, a high misdemeanor, and if the whole community should become involved in such
resistance would call down upon it the consequences of insurrection and
rebellion. I hope and trust that no such rash counsel will prevail. If,
unhappily, I am mistaken in this, I choose to shut my eyes to the consequences."

The timely advice contained in the recommendations of Governor Harding was not heeded. The people continued to violate the law with impunity. The
courts and the officials were powerless, under the Territorial Statutes, to enforce and execute the punitory provisions of the law. The anomalous condition of affairs
was presented of the will of the Nation being ignored
by a few men who claimed the sanction of Divine
authority for their acts. It is reported that the Mormons make the claim that they were led to believe by
National authority that the law of 1862 was not to be
enforced, but was to remain a dead letter on the statute
books. Certainly this was an error, and nothing but
the fact that the time of Congress was occupied with
matters involving the life of the Nation, and, after the
war, with other matters of importance, prevented

prompt and energetic action on the subject. Congress
has at every opportunity taken occasion in the most
signal manner to express its abhorrence of the practice
of polygamy. On June 23, 1874, the "Poland Act" became a law. It was the first law by which Congress had
struck at the judicial system under the cover of which
the Mormons had so long rendered the district courts
powerless. The jury panel was now to be selected by
the clerks of the district courts, and the probate judge
of the county in which the terms of court were held.
Two hundred·names were to be selected annually, 100
by each. The experiment of mixed juries proved a failure. The grand juries were about equally divided,
which rendered abortive all attempts to indict polygamists, In 1878 a partial relief came from an unex-
pected source. The Legislative Assembly passed an act
regulating the mode of procedure in criminal cases
which provided for challenges for actual bias to be tried
by triers appointed by the court. When the case of
Miles, indicted for polygamy, was reached for trial, the
District Attorney challenged the Mormon jurors for
actual bias, the court appointed triers, and the chal-
lenge was sustained. The Mormon Legislature has
practically adopted the California code, which contained
this provision, probably not anticipating such a construction by the court.

The act properly known as the "Edmunds Act" was
approved March 22, 1882. The penalty for polygamy
was made the same as that fixed by the laws of 1862. A
penalty was also provided "against any man who sim-
ultaneously, or on the same day, married more than one
woman." "Simultaneous" nuptials was an expedient
adopted to protect those who chose to violate the law.
The law further provided a penalty for unlawful cohabitation. Heretofore the law made the marriage a crime.
Now the living together, the holding out of two or more
women to the world as wives, was made a misdemeanor.

The great necessity for this amendment arose from the difficulty of securing the conviction of polygamists.

The entire Mormon community conspired to conceal the evidence of such marriages, until the statute of limitations would prove a bar to prosecution. Then the polygamous relation would be openly acknowledged. Before the passage of this act the Mormon leaders were frequently seen on the streets, in the theaters and other public places with their polygamous wives. The law also provided for amnesty to such offenders as would in good faith renounce polygamy. Eighty-one persons have thus far been amnestied by the President. The issue of polygamous marriages before January 1, 1883, were legitimated. The vital importance of making the continuance of the polygamic relation a misdemeanor is seen in the incipient contest which it has produced in the Mormon Church. At first several of the persons thus arraigned, promised in open court to obey the laws thereafter, and this in the face of strenuous opposition.

The *Deseret News*, the church organ, editorially proclaimed that no Mormon could consistently make such a promise without violating obligations which bound him for time and eternity. Those who did so were referred to in a manner calculated to make their neighbors feel that they had incurred disgrace. In the case of John Sharp, decisive action was taken. He was a prominent man in the Territory, a gentleman of high character, who had secured the respect of the people. He had the courage and the patriotism to appear in Court and announce his intention to obey the laws. He was promptly removed from the office of Bishop of the 20th Ward of Salt Lake City, in which office he had become endeared to the people by associations extending beyond a period of twenty years. It was thought that his patriotic course would have an influence upon others and encourage them to respect the law; hence the summary treatment he received.

[Marginal notes:] The Mormon community conspire to conceal evidence of polygamous marriages. / Amnesty provided for. / Number amnestied. / Incipitent contest in the Mormon Church. / Determined effort to prevent polygamists from promising to obey the law. / Case of John Sharp.

During the two years ending August 21st, 1887, but two or three persons, convicted of unlawful cohabitation, have promised to obey the law, to escape imprisonment.

At the September term, 1887, of the Third District Court, the first two persons convicted of unlawful cohabitation, promised to obey the law for the future. It is proper we should here say that an opportunity has always been given to these people by the Court, to escape punishment by a promise to obey the laws.

Since the passage of the Edmunds law of 1882, the following number of persons have been indicted and convicted for unlawful cohabitation and polygamy.

	No. Indicted.	No. Convicted.	
Unlawful Cohabitation	541	289	Number of convictions for polygamy and unlawful cohabitation.
Polygamy	27	14	
Total	568	303	

Many of the persons indicted have fled or have concealed themselves to escape arrest.

In the enforcement of the law the present officers of the Federal Courts in Utah are entitled to special commendation, and this should also include the late able and efficient prosecuting attorney. *Federal officers commended.*

While but a small proportion of the offenders have been convicted, the tension produced by these prosecutions cannot be over-estimated. Actuated by a determination not to recognize the supremacy of National laws where they forbid crimes sanctioned by a religious creed, it is not surprising that the leaders have resorted to unusual methods to defeat the law, and so great is their influence, and so compact their organization, that the entire membership have been a unit in aiding and abetting the offenders in their obstructive course, and in escaping the penalty of their crimes. The law of 1882 invites the Mormon people, through their Legislative Assembly, to bring Utah into harmony with the expressed will of the Nation; to recognize the fact that *Unusual methods resorted to by Mormons to defeat the law prohibiting polygamy.* *Invitation to the Mormon people to bring Utah into harmony with the Nation.*

every interest must remain subordinate to the general welfare, and be subject to the Constitution and the laws; to cease the wretched policy of evasion and resistance to law, which, if persisted in, will destroy the public pride and result in moral decay; and to correct the wrongs which have so long held Utah up to the public gaze in deplorable pre-eminence.

Recommenda-
tio is of Gov.
Murray.

Governor Murray in his message to the Legislative Assembly of 1884, the first after the passage of the Edmunds act of 1882, and again in 1886, called attention to the invitation to the Mormon people contained in the law, and expressed his willingness to co-operate with them in the adoption of proper measures.

Anti Polygamy
Laws in effective
operation for
about three years

The National laws relating to bigamy and polygamy have been in effective operation, for about three years. Standing face to face with the law, the leaders and their obedient followers have made no concession to its supremacy, and the issue is squarely maintained between assumed revelations and the laws of the land. As late as August 23rd, 1887, and seven weeks after the

Mormon leaders
have made no
concession to the
law prohibiting
polygamy

adoption of the proposed State Constitution, at Provo City, Utah, a public reception was tendered by the Mormon people at their meeting house, to several persons, polygamists, who had just been released from the penitentiary. Among the speakers were two of the stake presidency, two bishops and elders of the church, nearly all of whom were polygamists, and who proclaimed their intention to live in the future as they had in the past.

The two political
parties in the Territory.

The two elements of population are divided into the People's party (Mormon,) and the Liberal party (non-Mormon). Up to 1870, the Mormons had no opposition except in 1867, when a non-Mormon candidate for Delegate to Congress received 105 votes. The Liberal party was organized in 1870, and has continued to maintain its organization up to the present time. Its highest vote was polled for Philip T. Van Zile, candidate for Delegate

to Congress, at the first election held under the law of
March 22nd, 1882. He received 4884 votes against 23,-
039 for John T. Caine. This brings us down to the registration and election of 1887.

THE REGISTRATION AND ELECTION OF 1887.

The first annual election since the Act of Congress
prescribing a registration oath for voters was held on
August 1st, of this year, and was preceded by a registration under that act, made in the months of May and
June last. The Commission, after careful consideration,
to aid in securing uniformity of action by the registration officers, formulated and submitted to them for
their use, as an advisory act on the part of the Commission, a form of registration oath, substantially in the
words of the act, as follows:

Registration and
election of 1887.

TERRITORY OF UTAH, ⎫ ss.:
COUNTY OF.......... ⎭

I............ being duly sworn (or affirmed,) depose and say that I am
over twenty-one years of age, that I have resided in the Territory of Utah
for six months last past, and in this precinct for one month, immediately
preceding the date thereof; and that I am a native born or naturalized,
(as the case may be) citizen of the United States; that my full name is
.... that I am....years of age; that my place of business is
.... that I am a (single or) married man, that the name of my
lawful wife is.................... and that I will support the Constitution
of the United States, and will faithfully obey the laws thereof, and especially will obey the Act of Congress approved March 22, 1882, entitled, "An
act to amend Section 5352 of the Revised Statutes of the United States in
reference to bigamy and for other purposes," and that I will also obey the
Act of Congress of March 3, 1887, entitled "An Act to amend an Act entitled
An Act to amend Section 5352 of the Revised Statutes of the United Sta'es
in reference to bigamy and for other purposes. approved March 22, 1882,"
in respect of the crime in said act defined and forbidden, and that I will
not, directly or indirectly, aid or abet, counsel or advise any other person
to commit any of said crimes defined by Acts of Congress as polygamy,
bigamy, unlawful cohabitation, incest, adultery and fornication.

The Commission
oath.

Subscribed and swore to before to before me on this...day of.....188..
..............:......Deputy Registration Officer for..........Precinct......
County.

Although the person applying to have his name registered as a voter
may have made the foregoing oath, yet if the Registrar shall for reason-
able or probable cause, believe that the applicant is then. in fact, a big-

amist, polygamist, or living in unlawful cohabitation, incest, adultery or fornication, in our opinion the Registrar may require the applicant to make the following affidavit:

TERRITORY OF UTAH, }
COUNTY of.......... } ss.:

    I................further swear (or affirm) that I am not a bigamist, polygamist, or living in unlawful cohabitation, or associating or cohabiting polygamously with persons of the other sex, and that I have not been convicted of the crime of bigamy, polygamy, unlawful cohabitation, incest, adultery or fornication.

    Subscribed and sworn to before me on this........day of........188..
............Deputy Registration Officer for............Precinct..........
County.

    NOTE.—Those parts of the above form in relation to being "sworn or affirmed," and as to being a "native-born or naturalized citizen," and as to being a "single or married man," should be changed by *erasure*, or a line drawn through the words so as to be applicable to the case.

Address by the People's Party.

Prior to the registration, and under the date of April 4th, 1887, the Central Committee of the "People's" party, (Mormon) issued an address, advisory, to the voters of the party, in which the oath prescribed by the act was commented upon, interpreted and explained, and the voters informed that, as to male voters, there is nothing in the act which need necessarily reduce their numbers; that duty called them to wakefulness and activity, and all who could take the oath were urged to do so. The substance of the interpretation is in this extract:

    "The questions that intending voters need, therefore, ask themselves are these: Are we guilty of the crimes in said act; or, have we the present intention of committing these crimes, or of aiding, abetting, causing or advising any other person to commit them? Male citizens who can answer these questions in the negative can qualify under the existing laws, as voters and office holders."

An incorrect exposition of the law.

This interpretation does not seem to be a correct exposition of the law, and is well adapted to quiet the conscience of the voter and invite him to find his mind free from any intention relating to the subject. The clear meaning of the law is that the voter must have *a present, affirmative intention to obey the law in the future,* while the interpretation given by the "People's" party invites him to take the oath if he can merely say *he has not a present affirmative intention to violate the law.* The law prescribes a rule of action to bind the voter for the future which cannot be broken without subjecting him to the reproach of moral perjury.

When a law can be assumed to express the will and belief of a people subject to its provisions, those who have not formed the intention to violate it, may fairly be assumed to have the intention to obey it, and in such cases the distinction between an *actual* intent to obey, and a *formal* intent to disobey a law might not be of much practical importance, for a good citizen who had not formed an intention to violate the law, might well be assumed to have an intention to obey it. When, however, the law expresses neither the will nor the belief of a great majority of a people, the assumption of the intention to obey cannot be affirmed from the absence of a formal intention to disobey, and, like some other inviting ground, the field of *no intention* may be broad, and to those who may wish to occupy it, very desirable. The address was well calculated to invite the "intending voter" to silence the promptings of his conscience in relation to an institution which they claim is "interwoven with their dearest and earliest hopes connected with eternity," in favor of increasing the number of voters of the "People's party." The address further contained the remarkable statement that this was "not a time to indulge in 'bogus' sentiment."

Remarkable features of the address.

Members of the Liberal Party, in view of the evasive interpretation given by the Central Committee of the People's party, were not satisfied with the form of oath formulated by the Commission, and asked the Commission to recommend a form of oath which they claimed was necessary to bring the true intent and meaning of the law within reach of the conscience of the voter, as follows:

TERRITORY OF UTAH ⎰ ss.:
COUNTY OF........:. ⎱

I...............being duly sworn (or affirmed,) depose and say that I
am over twenty-one years of age, that I have resided in the Territory of
Utah for six months last past, and in this precinct for one month preceding the date hereof; and I am a native-born (or naturalized), as the case

Oath suggested
by non-Mormon
citizens.

may be, citizen of the United States; that my full name is...............;
that I am.... .....years of age; that my place of business is............;
that I am a (single or) married man; that the name of my lawful wife is
..............; that I will support the Constitution of the United States
and will faithfully obey the laws thereof; and I will especially obey the
acts of Congress prohibiting polygamy, bigamy, unlawful cohabitation,
incest, adultery and fornication; that I will not hereafter at any time,
within any Territory of the United States, while said acts of Congress
remain in force, in obedience to any alleged revelation, or to any counsel,
advice or command, from any person or source whatever, or under any
circumstances, enter into plural or polygamous marriage, or have or take
more wives than one, or cohabit with more than one woman; that I will
not at any time hereafter, in violation of said acts of Congress, directly or
indirectly, aid or abet, counsel or advise any person to have or to take
more wives than one, or to cohabit with more than one woman, or to
commit incest, adultery, or fornication; that I am not a bigamist or
polygamist; that I do not cohabit polygamously with persons of the other
sex, and that I have not been convicted of any of the offences above
mentioned.

Subscribed and sworn to before me this........day of...........188..
...............Deputy Registration Officer for..........Precinct........
County.

This request the Commission declined, in substance
holding the form previously recommended contained all
the requirments of the law, in the language of the law,
and that they did not feel authorized to recommend any
additions to that form.

The discussion settled nothing, but only brought
out more clearly that no test oath as to future conduct
is of any value to prevent infractions of the law. That

Effect of the dis-
cussion with re-
spect to the oath.

whether a law will or will not be violated is a matter
depending on motives and conditions which no test oath
can reach or remove, and the probabilities in the case
will be largely affected by the opinions of the person
and community in which he lives, as to whether the
law is constitutional, and morally just, and whether or
not the prohibited act is morally and religiously right
or wrong.

In all the election districts the form recommended
by the Commission was used by the Registration Officers, although the other form· was distributed by the
Loyal League, a non-Mormon organization. In one district the Registrar attempted to use the form suggested
by the Liberal Committee, but he was removed, and another appointed who used the Commission oath. In another district tne registrar claimed the right to ask
voters questions not contemplated by the law, and was
promptly removed.

Commission oath used throughout the Territory.

The form of oath suggested by members of the
Liberal party was first used in the Third District Court,
presided over by Chief Justice Zane, and is now used in
the District Courts, of the Territory for the qualification of jurors.

The "non-Mormon" oath used in the courts.

The total registration in the Territory was 20,585.
At the general election of the Territory held on August
1, 1887, there were 13,395 votes cast for the People's
party candidates, and 3255 votes for the Liberal party
candidates, for the Legislative Assembly.

The registration. Total vote.

The People's Party elected 10 Councilors and 21
members. The Liberal Party, 2 Councilors and 3
members. The Liberals, if they had registered and
voted their full strength, could have elected, at least,
one more member of the Council and 2 members of the
House. The total vote cast in the Territory for all
officers was 16,901.

Members elect.

The returns were canvassed by a board consisting
of five reputable persons, appointed by the Commission.
The total number of county, precinct and municipal
officers elected was 470.

Canvassing Board appointed.

THE MOVE FOR STATEHOOD.

The present year has been marked by proceedings
to form a constitution on which to demand admission
to the Union of States; the fourth attempt for that
purpose in the history of the Territory.

People's Party issue call for a convention.

Before the election, on June 16th, 1887, a call appeared signed by the chairman and secretary of the People's party (Mormon), calling upon the people of Utah, irrespective of party, creed, or class, to assemble in mass conventions in their respective counties, on June 25th, 1887, at 12, M., for the purpose of appointing delegates to a convention to be held at Salt Lake City, on the 30th day of June, 1887, to frame a constitution preparatory to an application to Congress for admission to Statehood.

Non-Mormons refuse to recog nize the call

The non-Mormons were distrustful of the move and unitedly declined to join the convention, or to recognize it. They gave as reasons for declining that in view of the past history of Utah it was a proper case for Congress, in accordance with the general rule, to say when the time for such a move had arrived, and by an enabling act give it authority when, how. and by whom the convention should be called, and how conducted; that they did not understand this sudden, and to them unannounced call; that the entire proceeding was carried out by the dominant party, and delegates chosen without regard to forms of election or disqualification of voters, without previous discussion and from wholly unauthorized sources; and above all they did not think the attitude of the great majority of the people of Utah towards the laws and authority of the general government had been such as to invite the full confidence of Congress in their fidelity to the laws and government, and to justify that body in granting sovereign Statehood.

The convention meet ; adopts provision for pun ishment of poly- gamy, etc.

The convention met, and with surprising unanimity adopted a proposed constitution, which declares bigamy and polygamy to be misdemeanors, and affixes punishments. It also provides that no further legislation shall be required to make or define these offences; that the provision is not amendable without the consent of Congress, and proclaims the separation of Church and State. The instrument is silent as to the offense of unlawful cohabitation.

The Mormons claim that having taken this action, the people ought not to be longer denied a voice in the conduct of their own affairs, and in the selection of officials to carry on the government ; that in a Territorial condition citizens are deprived of the rights and powers which are the strength and glory of American citizenship; that as a Territory they are excluded from participation in affairs that vitally concern them; that Utah has the population, the material interests, the intelligence, the stability and the regard for Republican* principles and institutions which are necessary to the establishment of a free and sovereign State; that the movement for Statehood was not sectiaran, partisan, or confined to any sectional interest; but that the call was broad and comprehensive, and included citizens of every creed and class; that the convention adopted a constitution in good faith, which is as liberal and fair and patriotic as that of any State; that it was the work of monogomous citizens acting in their capacity as citizens; that until it can be shown to be otherwise their action should be accepted in good faith, and the constitution should be judged by its plain language and terms; that the question of whether under the constitution the provisions against polygamy will be enforced by the officials of the proposed State is a question that must be left to the future, and that time alone will show; that every community proposing to come into the Union as a State must be given a fair opportunity to prove whether or not they will carry out the provisions of their charter; that they have never been accused of insincerity by any one who knows what they have endured rather than make promises they did not intend to keep; that the religion of the people should not be dragged into the consideration of measures which are purely political; that in answer to the assertion that, as a State, they will coutinue to build up their church, they claim the Mormon people have the consti-

tutional right to use every means not inconsistent with
the laws of the land to secure converts to their religious faith, unrestrained by any constitutional or legal
provision; that Congress has not the right to interpose
as a condition precedent to the admission of the proposed State, that any church shall cease preaching its
doctrines or endeavoring to make proselytes; that ad-
mitting there is no grant of power under which Congress may sanction an amendment to a State constitution, should Congress refuse to act, the constitution cannot be amended in respect of the offenses named; that
the proposed constitution does not presume to say that
the President or Congress shall exercise the powers
granted them, but leaves the matter to their discretion;
that a Territory as a matter of right is entitled to admission into the Union of States whenever it possesses
the necessary population, and has a constitution in harmony with republican institutions; that acting through
the only class of citizens who enjoy the privilege of the
elective franchise, the monogamous Mormons, they have
met the wishes of a Nation by a constitution which
provides for the punishment of those offences which
have excited the hostility of the Nation, and having
done so, they now ask to be allowed to hereafter control the affairs of the Territory, as the Constitution of
the United States intended they should; that the opposition to the admission of Utah as a State comes from
a class who have been the bitter and consistent enemies of the Mormon people, and who are inspired by
the hope of bringing the people, while in a Territorial
condition, within their power.

The above we believe to be a fair summary of the
reasons which the Mormons urge in favor of Statehood
for Utah.

The action of the convention and the result of its
labors did not tend to allay, but rather to increase, the
apprehensions and opposition of the non-Mormons.

They make many objections to the admission of Utah
as a State at present, and unanimously declined to vote
upon the subject,or in any way recognize the move. The
following is a summary of some of their objections:

That the action taken is without authority from
the proper source and not entitled to any recognition,
and accompanied by many and strong evidences of eva-
sion and bad faith in professing an abandonment of *Objections urged by non-Mormons*
polygamy and the accompanying social evils, with the *against the admission of Utah.*
intent to acquire Statehood, and without any intent to
restrain and puuish such offenses, but merely to entrench them behind Statehood; that the historical
attitude of the great body of the people towards the
laws on this subject had not changed down to the eve
of calling the convention, and that until then the Mormons, their press and pulpits, had not ceased to declare
the laws of Congress unconstitutional and their enforcement persecution; that though the press and pulpits
suddenly became silent, with indications in a few places
of a muzzled silence, there was still no sign or intima-
tion of any change of sentiment in words or acts, and
the hostility to the enforcement of existing laws and
Federal authority was still as active and general as
before; that scarcely any Mormon in good standing
would even promise to obey the laws in the future to
escape punishment after conviction in court; that they
were unable to understand how the great body of the
people could undergo an overnight conversion on the
subject of these offenses, when the day before their consciences were so strong that nothing could induce them
to promise obedience to the laws; that the *Deseret Evening News*, their leading and uncompromising organ, had,
after the framing of the proposed constitution, and
before the election, printed an editorial leaving the
question to the voters with the most judicial fairness,
but ending with the advice to be "as wise as serpents
and harmless as doves;" that in view of their past history

the first evidence of a *bona fide* intent to obey and execute laws making these offenses punishable should be a cessation of hostility to present laws and the announcement of obedience to them; that notwithstanding the great unanimity in the convention and in the subsequent vote of the people, no member of the convention, or voter, has in the constitution or elsewhere declared he considered or believed either of the offenses named is or should be a misdemeanor or punishable, but the provision in the constitution is introduced by the remarkable, whereas: for the reason that somebody, perhaps some wicked person at Washington, deems those crimes incompatible with a republican form of government, they are made misdemeanors and punishable; that it is not easy to conceive why the incompatibility should be limited to a republican form of government, or why it should not extend to every form of civilized government, unless full force is given to the dogma taught by the dominant sect, that the only true and rightful government is a theocracy in which the powers of government are derived from God and delegated to ministers, who govern by divine right; that no constitutional provision can execute itself, but requires prosecutors, jurors and judges, all of whom under Statehood would be Mormons, and if a whole people can be suddenly converted one way in one night, they might be susceptible to a reconversion equally sudden, and all the prosecuting powers become hostile to the law; that the rules of evidence and the laws of marriage under Statehood are proper subjects of State legislation, and while marriage without witnesses may be good, a rule of evidence that it requires one or more witnesses to the direct fact of marriage to commit polygamy would leave the constitutional provision worthless, and should the courts adopt the rule still existing in some States, that on a charge of bigamy, cohabitation and the repute of marriage are insufficient to prove the marriage, no new law or rule of evidence would be needed; that it is historical there are many polygamists in Utah, and as such marriages are concealed the number is unknown, and so far as the constitution is concerned, all these could live openly with their numerous families as soon as the Federal laws ceased, and point to their relations as the reward of those who had lived up to the privileges of their religion; that there is no grant of power in the constitution authorizing Congress to sanction or refuse an amendment to the constitution of a sovereign State; that the people of a State cannot deprive themselves of the power to amend a constitution the creation of their will, nor can they legislate to bind those that come after Same. them; that the Mormons have hitherto justified their opposition to the Federal laws under plea of conscience in respect to religious matters, but they have apparently made their consciences a marketable commodity and Statehood the exchangeable value, if they offer in good faith to suppress these offenses, unless their religious views have suddenly changed, of which there is no evidence or pretense; that the claim that this constitution emanates from and is the work of non-polygamous Mormons is no argument in its favor; that good citizenship does not involve only the question who in fact practices polygamy, but, also, who believes in it as a moral and religious right, superior to all human laws, and hence will be influenced in his conduct by such belief; that the non-polygamists have always been a large majority, but have in every way upheld the polygamists, have been equally active and bitter in their opposition to the laws, and without their aid and support the polygamists could not so long have defied the laws; that there has been no evidence of any struggle or contest between the polygamists and monogamists, but all have acted with the greatest possible harmony and vied with each other in attaining the wisdom of serpents and harmlessness of doves; that the church leaders who control in such matters have never manifested in any manner their intention to cease to enforce the practice of polygamy by their people, but that their silence indicates that the converse of the proposition is true; that the Mormon Church has never abandoned its purpose of ultimately becoming a controlling political power, and adopts this method of promoting it; and further, that if the non-polygamists have reached this conclusion, that the law in respect to these offenses is superior, and that it is the first duty of citizens to obey the laws of Congress prescribing rules of conduct, it is an easy manner for them to announce it and give some evidence of their good faith.

In accordance with these views the non-Mormons abstained from voting on the subject at the polls, desiring not to recognize the movement in any manner whatever.

Votes cast for the proposed constitution.

The monogamous Mormons cast 13,195 votes in favor of the constitution, 500 votes being cast against it.

The anomalous action of the Mormons.

The action of the Mormon people in adopting a constitution which forbids polygamy and bigamy, in view of their past history, is an anomaly which demands some explanation. In all its Territorial history, Utah, under the control of the dominant sect, which is in reality a polictical organization, with aims and methods which are political, has stood arrayed in opposition to laws of Congress on these subjects, and still maintains united efforts to nullify them.

Opinions and purposes of the Mormons.

To arrive at a fair conclusion of the opinons and purposes of the Mormon people with respect to polygamy, it is proper that the views and expressions of their press and pulpits should be considered.

The *Deseret News* in its issue of Oct. 6th, 1880, said:

Deseret News editorial.

"But we claim the right under the constitution of our country to receive just as many divine communications as the Almighty chooses to bestow and to follow these revelations without molestation or hindrance. At the same time it is our intention to abide by the laws of our country. When we refer to the laws of the land, we wish to be understood that we make one exceptiou, that is the law framed and pushed through Congress for the express purdose of preventing us from obeying a revelation from God, which we have followed in faith, and practiced for many years."

The claim thus made has been reiterated by the First Presidency of the Church from time to time. In their address of July 24, 1885, they said:

"We cannot, however, at the behest of men, lay aside those great prin- Address of the ciples which God has communicated to us, nor violate those sacred and First Presidency. eternal covenants which we have entered into for time and eternity."

Nothing has transpired to lead us to believe that No change in the the views thus expressed by their Church organ, and most people. views of the prominent leaders, are not entertained by the Mormon people to-day.

The call for assembling of mass meetings to appoint delegates to meet in convention and frame a constitution was evidently the result of a very sudden in- The sudden call spiration, so much so that the *Deseret News* editorially tion. Conventional said, "It would occasion some surprise." There had been no previous discussion in the press, nor among the people, in relation to such a movement, which was conceived and carried through with the utmost haste. Within fourteen days after the call was promulgated, delegates appointed to frame the constitution had met in convention.

The election of delegates to a constitutional convention by means of mass meetings does not commend itself to persons who have been accustomed to see the important duty of framing a constitution for a sovereign State, approached with care and deliberation, in accord with the general will of the people, and under proper authority, with no other aim and purpose than to advance the interests of all, and not of a particular class.

The provision in the constitution with reference to polygamy and bigamy is as follows:

SEC 12. Bigamy and polygamy being considered incompatible with The provision "a republican form of government," each of them is hereby forbidden and prohibiting poly- declared a misdemeanor. gamy.

Any person who shall violate this section shall, on conviction thereof, be punished by a fine of not more than $1000, and imprisonment for a term of not less than six months nor more than three years, in the discretion of the court. This section shall be construed as operative without the aid of legislation, and the offenses prohibited by this section shall not be barred by any statute of limitation within three years after the commission of the offense; nor shall the power of pardon extend thereto until such pardon shall be approved by the President of the United States.

Comparison between the proposed Constitution and the Federal law.

The crime of polygamy is to be a misdemeanor, (in every other State it is a felony), and is punishable by a fine of not more than $1,000.00, and by imprisonment for a term of not more than three years, whereas, under the Federal law, the fine is fixed at a sum not exceeding five hundred dollars, and imprisonment for a term not exceeding five years. Under the Federal law polygamists are denied the right to vote and hold office, but under this proposed constitution persons who have committed, or who shall hereafter commit, the crime of polygamy, and all such as continue to live in that crime, will be invested with the full rights of citizenship. Under the Federal law, unlawful cohabitation is punished by a fine not exceeding three hundred dollars, and by imprisonment for a term not exceeding six months; under the proposed State this offence, which perpetuates the evils of polygamy against society and posterity, is to go unpunished.

Limitation of the power of the Legislature.

The Legislature of the proposed State is shorn of its power to raise the grade of the crime to that of felony, or to annex any disqualification on conviction, while it is left free to promote polygamy by providing through inheritances and by means of wills for the maintenance of polygamous households, and to deny the legal wife the right of dower, or other rights, as heretofore.

Inoperative provision for amending constitution and pardoning polygamists.

The provisions for amendments to the proposed constitution, only by the consent of Congress, and for pardon of convicted polygamists only by approval of the President, are incongruous and futile, and need not be considered. It is sufficient to say they are open to the criticism that if a community cannot be trusted to amend a constitution it can hardly be said to be fit to be trusted with the powers of a State under any form of constitution, and if it cannot be trusted to deal with those who have violated its laws, it should not have the control of the administration of the laws.

If Utah should be admitted into the Union as a State, the following result would follow, viz.: There would be an immediate cessation of all further prosecutions for polygamy and unlawful cohabitation under laws of Congress. No prosecution for polygamy would ever take place in the State, until the ruling power in the State chose to do what they ` now arraign the Government for—"persecute" for a crime which is "an essential part of their religion." This claim has been set forth in a formal way which has made it a solemn declaration of the whole Mormon population of Utah. At a general conference held at Logan, April 6, 1885, a resolution was adopted and a committee appointed to draft a protest and address to the President and people of the United States. Such address was adopted at a mass meeting, held May 2, 1885, at which the Hon. John T. Caine, Delegate from the Territory, presided, and was deputed as the agent to present the same. In that document is formally proclaimed—

Results which will follow the admission of Utah.

"As to our religious faith, it is based upon evidence which to our minds is conclusive; convictions not to be destroyed by legislative enactments or judicial decisions. Force may enslave the body, but it cannot convince the mind. To yield at the demand of the legislature or judge the rights of conscience, would prove us recreant to every duty we owe to God and man. Among the principles of our religion is that of immediate revelation from God; one of the doctrines so revealed is celestial or plural marriage, for which ostensibly we are stigmatized and hated. This is a vital part of our religion, the decisions of courts to the contrary notwithstanding.''

Polygamy an essential part of Mormon religion.

It is a circumstance worthy of mention that Mr. Caine, who bore so prominent a part in the adoption and promulgation of the address from which the above extract was made, was also the president of the convention which adopted the proposed State constitution.

Under the proposed constitution no disqualification
would follow the commnision of those crimes; the right
of voting would be fully accorded to the ruling class
now disfranchised. No prosecution would ever take
place for continuing that crime, by living in unlawful
cohabitation, and multiplying its fruits to the degrada-
tion of posterity. The right of dower created by Congress would be swept away. The Utah policy has ever
been to deny that right to the legal wife, and make her
right depend upon the testamentary disposition of her
husband. The rights of the minority population would
be left to the mercy of a majority, who regard them as
intruders, and who have always used political power in
a clannish spirit. In illustration of their spirit in such
matters a statement of their course in the election of
officers for the Deseret University and Territorial Insane
Asylum will suffice. The university was incorporated
when the Territory was first organized, and although
some fifteen officers, chancellor and regents, are elected
biennially to manage this educational institution, which
receives support from the Territorial Treasury, not one
representative of the minority has ever been elected.
For the Insane Asylum, built by an appropriation from
the Territorial Treasury, a certain number of directors
are elected biennially, but the minority have never
been accorded a representative, a privilege and a right
which is recognized in every other Territory or State.
Further, in Salt Lake City, where the minority have a
majority in two of the five organized precincts, they are
denied any representation in the city council, by reason
of an election law which requires all the city officers to
be elected on a common ticket.

The Mormon people cannot be called hypocrites.
They boldly proclaim their religious belief to all the
world. Until that belief shall be changed if they be
true to their creed, polygamy with its kindred evils will
be fostered by every means in their power. The leaders

Margin notes: No disqualification for polygamy nor prosecution for unlawful cohabitation. Dower would be swept away. The rights of the minority would be ignored. The Mormon policy in this respect. Mormon efforts to enforce polygamy.

of the church will probably do in the future what they have done in the past. They do not recognize the authority of the Government to call upon them for any support in its contest with polygamy, but they do recognize the divine command to encourage polygamy. The attitude, purpose and determination of the church in this respect has been fully developed. In the case of W. W. Taylor, son of John Taylor, who died a few years ago, it was acknowledged after his death that he was a polygamist, and yet he held a responsible office under the city government of Salt Lake City up to the time of his death. Another case was that of Jos. H. Dean; he was elected and served as a member of the city council of Salt Lake. While in office it was learned that he was, and had been a polygamist for over three years. The leaders of the church had full knowledge of the fact that these men were disqualified from holding office under the Federal law, yet they acquiesced in their unlawful occupancy of public offices. We have learned of similar cases in the more remote counties. The non-polygamist Mormons were also aware that the men referred to were polygamists, and their course has been in harmony with that of their leaders, as it will probably always be. During the period in which the government has been actively engaged in prosecuting offenders, they have unitedly refused to extend any aid, but have denounced the prosecutions as persecution.

The Church encourages the unlawful occupancy of public office.

Non-polygamist Mormons support the polygamists.

For these reasons the Commission has been led to fear that the provision in the proposed Constitution making polygamy a misdeamor was not adopted, nor the action taken with any purpose to suppress polygamy; that it does not indicate an abandonment by the people of Utah in the manner which is demanded by the will of the American people, as expressed in their National law; that the late movement for Statehood was the offspring of necessity, inspired with the hope of escaping from the toils which the firm attitude of the govern-

The action taken not an abandonment of polygamy.

ment and the energetic course of the Federal officers
had wound around them. Realizing that they could
expect no aid nor comfort from the National administration, and actuated by a determination not to recognize
the supremacy of National laws where they forbid crimes
licensed by their creed, it is not surprising that the
majority in Utah should resort to some expedient to get
relief from their dilemma. In the light of these facts
it is evident that the relief sought for is expected in
Statehood, and that this expedient is, in the case of
Utah, inspired by more than the usual motives operating
in other communities, which are composed of homogeneous American population in accord with the laws and
institutions of the country.

The presentation of the proposed application for
Statehood will demand the consideration of the question
by Congress, whether the course of the dominant
majority in Utah, in the use of delegated powers in a
Territorial condition, has been such as to induce
Congress to withdraw certain of these powers until the
perpetuated evil should be corrected, (which has not
been done).

If Utah, as a Territory, has refused to recognize the
force and validity of National laws, and decisions of the
Supreme Court, can it be reasonably expected as a State
it will do so? Can it be reasonably expected that crimes
and evils which the government has failed to suppress
with its supervision over a Territorial Government, will
be suppressed in a State ruled by the majority which
now maintains and propagates these crimes and
evils as "an essential part of their religion."

It is submitted if it would not be wise to continue
a Territorial government in which the National government could continue to deal directly with those evils
until they should be eradicated, even if it should be
necessary, as suggested in former reports of 1884-5 to
take all political power from those who have not suffic-

ient allegiance to recognize the validity of National
laws and the decisions of courts, and that no harmony
in the Union could be maintained with a State ruled by
a creed, which claims all governments but its own to be
illegal, and claims a "separate political destiny and
ultimate temporal dominion and by divine right."

The Commission is of the opinion that Utah should
not be admitted to the Union until such time as the
Mormon people shall manifest by their future acts that
they have abandoned polygamy in good faith, and not
then until an amendment shall have been made to the
Constitution of the United States prohibiting the practice of polygamy. We append to this report resolutions
adopted by the Presbyterian and Methodist churches of
Utah. *Utah should not be admitted until polygamy has been abandoned in good faith.*

POLYGAMOUS MARRIAGES.

The names of sixty-seven men have been reported
to the Commission who have entered into polygamy
during the year ending June, 1887. This information
has been requested of all registrars. The number given
has been reported by non-Mormon registrars, there
being no instance in which a name has been reported
by a Mormon registrar. *Number of polygamous marriages.* The law imposes upon
the Commission the duty of appointing proper
persons to perform the important duty of regis-
tering voters, and it has been the uniform policy of the
Commission in filling these offices to select men, whenever they could be found, who were in open and avowed
sympathy with the law under which they were acting. *Class of persons appointed Registration officers.*
The necessity for this is apparent. The registration
officers are charged with the duty of excluding from the
lists of voters at the annual registration in May and
June, and the annual registration in September, the
names of such persons as have entered into polygamy.
Under the Utah law the registry list continues from
year to year, only a revision is made by the registrar;
therefore, unless he is disposed to give full force and

— 46 —

effect to the provision of the law which disfranchises polygamists, this vital principle of the law may be utterly disregarded.

LEGISLATIVE APPORTIONMENT.

Legislative apportionment.

Under the act of March 3rd, 1887, the Governor, Utah Commission, and the Secretary of the Territory, were appointed a board to reapportion the Territory for Legislative representation. The board met and organized, and after careful consideration, reapportioned the Territory into twenty-four representative and twelve council districts, and under which the present Legislative Assembly was elected.

RECOMMENDATIONS.

The annual registrations.

The Commission was first organized in the summer of 1882. Its first duty was to adjust the local laws to the act of Congress, and to provide the necessary rules and regulations for conducting the registration and the election. Under its supervision a new registration was made in 1882, and again in 1887, under the Edmunds-Tucker act. Annual revisions were also made in 1883, 1884, 1885 and 1886. No person living in the practice of polygamy was allowed to register or to vote, and we believe that in this respect the purpose of the law has been thoroughly and effectually accomplished. The total registration in 1882 was 33,266; in 1883, 37,062; in 1884, 41,858; in 1885, 43,646; in 1886, 45,375. The registration of 1887, under the operation of the test oath, was 20,790. The elimination of the female vote will largely account for the difference, and there was a considerable percentage of voters who refused to take the oath prescribed by the act. Of these the larger proportion were probably non-Mormons.

The Commission in its previous reports, made since 1882, has made the following recommendations, which, in its opinion were needed to give force and effect to the provisions of the law under which it was created:

(1) The enactment of a marriage law.

(2) Making the first or legal wife a competent witness in prosecutions for polygamy.

(3) Restoring to the first or legal wife the right of dower as at common law, or other interests in the real estate, as provided in the statutes of many of the States.

(4) That provision be made for a fund, to be furnished by the Department of Justice to the proper legal authorities in the Territory.

(5) The conferring upon the United States Commissioners concurrent jurisdiction with the justices of the peace in civil and criminal matters.

(6) The appointment of the Territorial auditor, treasurer, commissioners to locate university lands, of the probate judges, county clerks, county selectmen, county assessors and collectors, and county superintendents of district schools, by the Governor of the Territory, subject to confirmation by the Commission.

(7) Authorizing the selection of jurors by *open venire*, especially in cases prosecuted by the United States.

(8) Giving to the district courts, jurisdiction of all cases of polygamy wherever in the Territory the crime may have been committed.

(9) That the Territorial courts in United States cases be invested with a power coextensive with that possessed by the United States circuit and district courts in the States in the matter of contempt and the punishment thereof.

(10) That prosecutions for polygamy be exempted from the operation of the general limitation laws.

(11) Authorizing the process of subpœna in all cases prosecuted by the United States, to run from the Territorial courts into any other district of the United States.

(12) That provision be made for binding over witnesses on the part of the Government in all United States cases to appear and testify at the trial.

(13) That when a continuance is granted upon motion of the defendant, provision should be made for taking deposition of witnesses on the part of the Government, the defendant to be confronted with the witness and to cross-examine. The deposition to be used in case of death, absence from Territory, or of the concealment of witness so as to elude process of subpœna.

(14) That it be made a penal offense for any woman to enter into the marriage relation with a man knowing him to have a wife living and undivorced. This should be coupled with a provision that in cases where the polygamous wife is called as a witness in any prosecution for polygamy against her husband, her testimony could not be used in any future prosecution against her, with a like provision as to the husband.

(15) That the term of imprisonment for unlawful cohabitation fixed by section 2 of the act of 1882 be extended to at least two years for the first and three years for the second offense.

(16) That all persons be excluded by law from making a location or settlement upon any part of the lands of the United States who shall refuse on demand to take and subscribe an oath, before the proper officer of the land office in which his or her application is made, that he (if a man) does not cohabit with more than one woman in the marriage relation, and that he will obey and support the laws of the United States in relation to bigamy or polygamy, or (if a woman) that she does not cohabit with a man having more than one living and undivorced wife, and that she will obey and support the laws of the United States in relation to bigamy and polygamy.

(17) That the laws with reference to the immigration of Chinese and the importation of contract laborers, paupers and criminals be so amended as to prevent the immigration of persons claiming that their religion teaches and justifies the crime of polygamy, as this would cut off the chief source of supply to the Mormon Church.

(18) A suggestion in favor of a constitutional amendment prohibiting polygamy.

Of these recommendations the 1, 2, 3, 5, and 12 have received the approval of Congress and are now part of the statute law.

We again respectfully recommend to the attention of Congress all of the above recommendations which have not yet received its approval.

The Commission recommends as a measure of great

Important recommendations. importance, the passage of a law conferring upon the Governor of the Territory, the authority to appoint the following county officers: Selectmen, Clerks, Assessors, Recorders and Superintendents of District Schools. This will place the control of county affairs, including the assessment of property, (but not the collection of revenue), and the supervision of the public schools, in the hands of persons in sympathy with the efforts of the government to extirpate polygamy. It will also strengthen the element in the different counties which is disposed to assist the Federal officers in their efforts to enforce and execute the laws. We also reccommend the passage of an act creating a board to consist of the Governor, Utah Commission, and Territorial Secretary to apportion Salt Lake City into aldermanic and council districts. Under the present law these officers are elected on a common ticket, thus denying the principle of precinct or ward representation, which obtains in other towns and cities.

The non-Mormon citizens of the Territory, acting through their political organizations, Democratic, Republican and Liberal, have repeatedly given expression to the opinion that the solution of the Mormon problem will be speedily and effectually accomplished by creating a Legislative Commission, to be appointed by the President, and to be confirmed by the Senate. In support of their position they urge the following reasons: That a republican form of government has no existence in Utah, the church being supreme over all; that until the political power of the Mormon Church is destroyed, the majority will not yield a full obedience to the laws, and only by providing a new code of laws, can they be compelled to do so; that common prudence suggests there should be no delay in taking from the Mormon Church the power to control in political matters; that this object can best be accomplished by providing an agency which is in accord with the purposes and will of the National Government; that the Legislative Assembly of the Territory has always been the creature of the church, and during its thirty-six years of existence has made a record which is impressive by its silence with respect to the passage of such laws as the government had the right to expect; that such an agency would relieve Congress from the consideration of the affairs of Utah; that Congress having the right to legislate directly for the Territories, which right has been affirmed by the Supreme Court, ought, in consideration of the extraordinary condition of affairs in the Territory, follow the precedents established in the case of Louisiana and of Florida, and grant a Commission; that such action will result in bringing Utah into harmony with the other State and Territories of the Union.

In conclusion, we respectfully submit that in our opinion, the results which have followed from the pas-

Reasons advanced by non-Mormons in favor of a Legislative Commission.

Salutary effects of the Edmunds Law. sage of the Edmunds Act, have been very beneficial to the Territory. It has provided a fair, honest and orderly system of elections, and it is universally conceded by Mormon and non-Mormon that there has been no charge nor even rumor of fraud in connection with the registration of voters and the conduct of elections since the Commission first commenced its work.

Very respectfully,

G. L. GODFREY,

A. B. WILLIAMS,

ARTHUR L. THOMAS.

HON. L. Q. C. LAMAR,
    Secretary of the Interior,
        Washington, D. C.
ST. LOUIS, Mo.

Commissioners Carlton and McClernand dissenting from some of the views expressed above, do not sign this report.

APPENDIX.

Resolutions adopted at the General Conference of the Methodist Church of Utah, held at Mt. Pleasant, Utah, August 8, 1887.

STATE OF AFFAIRS IN UTAH.

Each year develops new features in this field, which call for intense watchfulness on the part of all who are loyal to the Nation and its laws, and to the advancement of our Christian civilization in this Territory, and which demand the outspoken sentiments and efforts of all Christian organizations in meeting the spirit of Antichrist reigning here.

We therefore take as a keynote of our work the words of the Psalmist, "They that love the Lord HATE evil."

We declare in favor of a rigorous enforcement of the laws and the prosecution of all offenders as necessary to the eradication of the evils dominant here.

We enter our unqualified protest against the efforts now being made by the Mormons to secure Statehood for Utah, believing the proposed constitution to be a well-devised instrument to blind the people of this Nation to the real object in view, viz.. the perpetuation of the evil itself.

This constitution was framed by a convention of delegates appointed by mass meetings composed exclusively of Mormons. All the delegates were Mormons, and their action was entirely without the sanction or co-operation of the non-Mormon part of our population, and therefore was not in harmony with our republican ideals of representative action.

It being true that the Mormon community still hold to the divinity of polygamy and also still claim that all laws enacted by Congress for its suppression are unconstitutional; we therefore insist that the action to secure Statehood is inconsistent, and should be met by a strong and united opposition of the people of the United States through their Representatives in the National Congress. We urge upon our churches in the East to raise their voices against this new feature of Mormon duplicity.

APPEAL TO THE PRESBYTERIAN CHURCH

From the Presbytery of Utah, in session at Manti, August 28, 1887.

Affairs have reached a crisis in Utah. After years of defiance and determined evasion of the laws. a very plausible policy has been adopted by the Mormon leaders. A Constitutional Convention has been called, a constitution has been framed and submitted to the Mormon people and adopted by them. In this constitution is a clause making polygamy a crime, to be punished by fine and imprisonment.

This is the pretext by which they hope to deceive Congress, and to gain admission as a State. Professing to give up this objectionable feature of their religion, viz., polygamy, they now ask for Statehood.

We call attention to the following facts, which fully indicate the purpose of such action:

1. The so-called revelation on polygamy stands yet unrepealed by any authority from the church; it is, therefore, as binding as ever upon the whole Mormon people.

2. Up to the very meeting of this Constitutional Convention men brought before the courts refused to promise to obey the laws against polygamy, and are yet being arrested for the same crime, and yet refusing to obey.

3. Up to the present day any Mormon who promises to obey the laws against polygamy, is considered a traitor to his religion and is treated as such.

4. This movement for Statehood is altogether a Mormon movement. The Gentiles have taken no part in it, and are now a unit against it.

5. The Mormon people are as firm believers in polygamy to-day as they ever have been; they have no disposition to give it up; but through a strange policy recently adopted, they have made this sacred tenet of their religion a crime, whilst yet believing in its divine origin.

In view of these facts we, in common with other loyal citizens of Utah, do most earnestly protest against this whole movement, for the following reasons:

1. Because there is no sincerity in it. It is a fact well known to us who are here, and admitted to be such by many Mormons, that the real intention is not to abolish polygamy, but to obtain Statehood, get entire control of affairs in Utah and thus defeat the execution of the laws. For with Mormon judges, officers and jurors, no law against polygamy would be enforced. Hence this constitutional clause against polygamy is only a blind.

2. Because it would leave the power of the priesthood untouched. The twenty-five men to whom absolute obedience is pledged on the part of the people, would only be intrenched in their present stronghold.

3. Because it would be a death blow aimed at our American homes; it would check our Christian work, and give up forever this entire Territory to Mormon rule and policy.

4. Because the whole scheme means treason against the Government and its laws.

We therefore call upon the ministers and members of the Presbyterian Church, North and South, to raise their voices in protest against this religio-political chicanery.

GOVERNOR WEST ON STATEHOOD.

During the past year there have been three convictions for polygamy, and one hundred and fifty-seven for unlawful cohabitation.

CONSTITUTIONAL CONVENTION AND STATEHOOD.

I had occasion in my last annual report to set forth the situation here as follows:

The all-absorbing question in this Territory, dominating all others, hurtfully affecting its prosperity, impeding its advancement, and disturbing the quiet and happiness of its people, and the one question of the utmost concern and solicitude to the whole country, is the attitude of defiance assumed and maintained by the Mormon people, who probably are five-sixths of the whole population, to the law of Congress for the suppression of polygamy, known as the "Edmunds law." In all questions affecting the Mormon Church and people, the polygamous and monogamous Mormons make common cause, stand together, and are united. They maintain publicly through their leaders and teachers, in their houses of worship, through their press, and privately in social and business circles, that the law is infamous, an interference with, and a denial to them of that religious freedom guaranteed to all by the Constitution; of their right and religious duty to continue in violation of the law their polygamous relations, and they deny the authority of Congress to regulate and interpose any restrictions as to the marital relation; that the obedience which they owe and will cheerfully render to a power higher than any earthly power compels them to exercise their religious rights and privileges in

the face of and in violation of the law; that they are
prepared to, and will if required of them, sacrifice their
personal comfort, their property, suffer infinite imprisonment, and surrender life itself rather than yield and
promise obedience to the law and forego the privileges
they claim. The Government can have and hold but
one position towards this people, which is of easy statement. Its authority must be respected, its laws must
be obeyed.

It is true, however, that a large majority of the
people stoutly and stubbornly affirm, publicly and privately, that the enforcement of certain laws is destructive of their rights as freemen, an assault upon their religion, and an invasion of the sanctity of their homes.
The minority with equal vigor and openness proclaim
that the practices of those people are immoral; that
they are disloyal to the government, and their attitude
of defiance to the laws interferes with the advancement
and prosperity of the Territory,and inflicts injury upon
all of its interests.

It follows necessarily that the people here with a
bitterness of feeling are divided as they are nowhere
else in the country. The division is clear, distinct and
palpable.

The causes of division, in language not distin-
guished for its mildness, are constantly, earnestly, and
vehemently discussed through the press, in the houses
of worship, and in the social circle, engendering an intense feeling of bitterness. The vigorous enforcement
of the unpopular laws against the people in the majority, with a prospect of further stringent legislation,
does not tend to soothe or make them more amiable.

I then recommended the enactment by Congress of
the Senate Bill, as amended and reported from the Judiciary Committee of the House, entitled "An Act to
Amend an Act Entitled 'An Act to Amend Section
5352 of the Revised Statutes of the United States in

reference to bigamy and for other purposes,' " approved
March 22nd, 1882, as healthful and wise legislation for
the improvement of, and an aid to the final settlement
of our troublesome condition. Congress saw fit to make
important modifications of said bill before enacting it.
But a little more than six months have elapsed since
the bill became a law, yet within that short period a
material and wonderful change has taken place in the
situation here. Almost the entire adult Mormon population, except actual polygamists, have professedly
yielded the position heretofore maintained by them, and
held when my last report was made, and have taken
and subscribed to the oath, prescribed by law to qualify
themselves as electors and office holders.

[Here follow Commissioners' oath and an account
of the calling of the convention, the invitations to the
central committees to join and replies, all of which are
published herewith.]

THE STATEHOOD MOVEMENT.

It will be observed that the movement for Statehood was inaugurated by the leaders of the Mormon
people. Their representatives alone took part in the
deliberations of the convention, and that portion of the
people of the Territory only favor and support it. When
we remember how recently those people avowedly held
and maintained a position which placed them in opposition with the Federal laws, the holding of which in the
past had brought them into conflict with the people
with whom they lived in Ohio, Missouri and Illinois, and
in antagonism with all comers to this Territory not
identified with them; when we recall that a failure to
yield that position would have cost them the political
control, which they have held since the organization of
the Territory; that the securing of Statehood will place
in their hands, and take from Congress the power that
it has been compelled to exercise to regulate and control their actions in accordance with the moral sense

of the country and Christian civilization; before cloth-
ing them with sovereignty should not Congress wait
until the action is suited to the word, until their laud-
able professions have had time to ripen into praise-
worthy works, until the conduct of the people and the
legislation of the Territory in consonance with their
professions are brought into harmony with the general
views of the country, and the Territory placed in the
advanced position it would have attained but for the
past attitude of those who are now asking the boon of
Statehood?

In discussing and acting upon matters relative to this
Territory, it is too often the case that it is forgotten
that any other than our Mormon fellow citizens are
residents here. I know that it has been earnestly and
persistently urged, that the non-Mormons of this Territory are a set of political adventurers, who by constant
agitation and appeals to religious bigotry and prejudice,
have sought to incite the enmity of the country against
the majority, that they might obtain political power and
the opportunity to plunder and rob the Territory. It is
not true that the non-Mormons are of the character
stated, or that they seek by any means to accomplish
the purpose charged. Accordingly to their nuuber they
will compare favorably with any people in our land, and
have, I suppose, fewer political adventurers among them
than any portion of the country; the absence of induce-
ment making this necessarily so, as it is a fact easy of
ascertainment and patent to every observer, that since
the organization of the Territory, under past conditions,
they have never stood any chance of political preferment.
The minority portion of our population have been drawn
here by an inviting climate, a rich and attractive country, with a view to the acquiring of wealth and the
enjoyment of the comforts and blessings of life. They
number in their ranks, members of all the professions,
Bankers, Manufacturers, Merchants in all lines of busi-

ness, Farmers, Stockraisers, Miners, Mechanics, Laborers,
and representatives of the various industrial pursuits.
They have established great business enterprises, acquired much property and wealth, and are interested
alike with our Mormon population in the peace, prosperity and happiness of the Territory. It is true they
have with great unanimity vigorously opposed the
majority in the upholding of and the practice of polygamy, and earnestly combatted the Government of the
State by the church, maintained the supremacy of the
law and the duty of the citizen to obey it, and opposed
priestly dictation in secular affairs. I have yet to know
or hear of any one of this class who favors the admission now of Utah as a State.

The legislation of the last Congress for the benefit
of this Territory, having established confidence outside
of Utah, that the vexed question here would be settled,
and the determined effort inaugurated by our business
men to push forward the development of the Territory,
have already accomplished much good. Capital from
abroad has been invested in the purchase of real estate
in this and other cities of the Territory, purchasers are
still looking and buying, and there is an activity in the
real estate market unknown here for years. From
knowledge obtained by communication with investors
and those who are familiar with real estate operations,
I have a firm conviction, that a well grounded fear of
the admission of Utah as a State would stay our incom-
ing tide of prosperity, and lose us the already enhanced
and increasing values of our real estate.

It is more than probable, that the question of Utah
as a political factor in National affairs will be considered
in connection with the application for its admission as
a State. Neither of the great political parties. Democratic or Republican, so far as the past history of this
people is concerned, can lay claim with any degree of
certainty to their support. Their political history in the

States is known; also, the fact that always in this Territory, they have constituted a separate and distinct party, having their own organization independent of the Democrats and Republicans, and that all efforts to draw them from their own into another party have proven signal failures. They elect officers from their own numbers, because they are Mormons, without reference to their being either Democratic or Republican.

That the majority of this people have publicly proclaimed the abandonment of practices that put them at variance with the country at large, is matter of congratulation. A faithful adherence to the declarations now made by them means a settlement of the long-vexed question here, and can but inure to the prosperity and happiness of this people.

Very respectfully, your obedient servant,

CALEB W. WEST, Governor.

Hon. L. Q. C. Lamar,
    Secretary of the Interior.

THE NEW CONSTITUTION.

In determining the question whether the time is at hand when Utah should be admitted as a State, a very important consideration is involved. This is, are the people of the Territory dealing with the country at large, honestly and in good faith ? In this article, it is proposed to advance some few reasons, which indicate that under the present application is masked the same hostility to free institutions, and the same opposition to the restraints of wholesome laws, which has always marked the history of this strange people.

It is claimed by the advocates of Statehood for Utah, that the instrument presented for the consideration of the Congress of the United States, is unobjectionable in its provisions; and that the penal prohibition against polygamy found in Section 12, Article 15, is binding upon the people of the future State for all time, and therefore that it is a sufficient guaranty of the good faith and purpose of the Mormon people. It is not perceived that the provision of Section 1, Article 16, requiring the consent of Congress to any revision, change or amendment to Section 12, Article 15, adds any force to the argument.

The people of Utah have no power to barter or surrender their right of local self-government. Neither can they bind themselves nor those who shall succeed them, by irrevocable legislation. These propositions will not be controverted by any person who has reflected upon the constitutional and political relations of the several States to each other, and to the general Government. The questions, then, remain: are the people who

have presented this Constitution for the approval of
Congress, sincere in their professions apparently made
in this instrument, and have they honestly determined
to overthrow the very corner stone of the faith which
has so long fettered them? These questions must be
resolved by an analysis, in part at least, of the instrument itself, in the light of past and present history.

For nearly forty years the Church through its priesthood, has taught the people, that the regulation of the
marriage relation belongs exclusively to ecclesiastical
authority, and any interference by the State therewith,
is an unconstitutional usurpation of power. So long
ago as 1851, the General Assembly of the *State of Deseret*,
enacted [C. L. Utah p. 233.] an ordinance purporting to
have the effect of law, which incorporated all of the
inhabitants of the *State* (?) who were Latter-Day Saints,
as the Church of Jesus Christ of Latter-day Saints. Said
ordinance declared that said church " holds the constitutional and *original* right," among other things " to
solemnize marriage *compatible with the revelation* of Jesus
Christ." And further—

"That the said Church does, and sh‹ll possess and enjoy continually,
the power and authority, *in and of itself*, to originate, make. pass, and
establish rules, regulations, ordinances, laws, customs, and criterions, for
the good order, safety, government, convenience, comfort and control of
said church, and for the punishment or forgiveness of all offences relative
to fellowship, according to church covenants."

The reasons given for these extraordinary grants
of power, were, as stated in the ordinance—

"That the pursuit of bliss, and the enjoyment of life, in *every capacity*
of public association and domestic happiness, *temporal* expansion, or spiritual increase upon the earth, may not *legally* be questioned."

Further provision was that the church should keep a
record of all marriages, births and deaths. This is the
only law relative to marriage and its solemnization,
which the legislature of the Mormon people has ever
deemed proper to enact.

The reason is found in the belief of the people that
marriage is a sacrament, and that its solemnization and

regulation are divinely ordained, and by direct revelation the command of God has been communicated to them. In short, the doctrines and teachings of the church relative to marriage, are tenets of their faith, and, as they say, a part of their religious belief. It is this deeply rooted and widespread conviction, which has prompted their determined and defiant opposition to the laws prohibiting polygamy, which they claim to be in violation of the Constitution. Never, for a moment, have they renounced this position. The teachings of the church expounding the revelation concerning plural or polygamous marriage have also intimate relation with another tenet of the faith, which must also be considered in determining the question of good faith.

The doctrine in brief is, as the writer heard it expounded by George Q. Cannon and Charles W. Penrose, that there are numberless souls or spirits *in esse*, which can not be fully saved, unless they be born on the earth, and descend into the grave and thence be resurrected. That it is the highest duty of man and woman to bring as many children as possible into being, each child being the medium of passing to the higher exaltation one of these spirits. That the greatest enjoyment and exaltation in the life hereafter are reserved for those who beget and bear the most children, and consequently, that the bringing forth of children is one of the highest duties in life. As this purpose can not be fully subserved by man in his marriage union with one woman, patriarchal or plural marriage is commanded by God, and enjoined by the priesthood, as a religious *duty*. Now, in the light of this religious belief, which is reflected from every act in the history of this people, what just reason is there for concluding that the alleged surrender of religious principle, contained in the proposed Constitution, is made in good faith ? If this people believes the anti-polygamy legislation of Congress to be contrary to the law of God, what must they think of a similar enactment to be inserted in their own organic law ?

By their present application, assuming it to be made
in good faith, they affirm to the world, that the religious
convictions of a life time have been destroyed, and that
they stand ready to surrender for the sake of temporal
power one of the most sacred tenets of their faith.

A change, so unusual and unprecedented in history,
will not impress the ordinary mind with the conviction
of attendant sincerity, in the absence of explanation. Particularly is this true, since we see no practical change
in the attitude of the Mormon people toward the Federal
Government. So far as known no effort is or has been
made, by the people themselves, to enforce the laws
against polygamy and cohabitation with more than one
woman. Offenders against those laws still refuse future
obedience thereto, proudly leaving the criminal's dock
with the declaration, that they have no promises to make.

From their pulpits and tripods, the same prayers for
vengeance upon the government and all Americans who
have dared to question their acts, are directed to God,
and through their religious press, disseminated among
the people.

The whole Territory is to-day in the attitude of
opposing the laws of the land.

Let us approach the consideration of the questions
involved, then, bearing in mind the *fact,* that there is no
evidence of any change of conviction, or of purpose
even, shown by this people, save such as may be found
in the instrument presented for the people, by a number of *priests,* who, the Church organ aptly says, were
acting in their *political,* not their religious capacities.

Let us see, therefore, what evidence the proposed
Constitution itself affords.

The prominent declaration in that instrument is—

"SEC. 12. ART. 15: Bigamy and polygamy being considered incompatible with a republican form of government, each of them is hereby forbidden and declared a misdemeanor."

The framers of the instrument have very carefully
omitted to include in the foregoing clause, a prohibi-

tion against *patriarchal, plural* or *celestial* marriages. This omission becomes significant when it is considered that the church makes a broad distinction between bigamy or polygamy and the patriarchal, plural or celestial marriage authorized by its creed. Bigamy, say the Mormon priests, is a crime against the wife and against God:

The taking of a second wife by a man not a member of the Mormon Church, nor a believer in its doctrines, is a violation of the contract with the wife, and being against her will, is criminal. It is an offense against God, because He has only granted the privilege of plural marriage to his own people, and only upon condition that the true wife consents. This consent in many instances is inferred from her marriage vows, in others, is expressly given or extorted, but in every case, (they say) is a pre-requisite to a valid plural marriage. Plural or celestial, also called patriarchal marriage, say they, wrongs no one. All of the parties in interest consent, and it is in accordance with divine law.

Such marriages are not bigamous nor polygamous in the sense of the laws prohibiting bigamy and polygamy. In fine, they make and declare a clear distinction between bigamy or polygamy as understood and defined in the laws of all civilized States, and their own plural or celestial marriage.

In the light of this distinction, they are willing to provide penalties for offenses which could only be committed by persons not of their faith. Let us look a little further. There is no *prohibition* against cohabitation with more than one woman. The living together as man and wife with all of the usual and ordinary consequences, is the practical result of marriage, monogamous or polygamous. This *practical* relation of polygamous marriage is just as detrimental to the interests of society as the act by which the marriage *status* is created. In this view Congress has heretofore prohibited by stringent legislation the continuance of polygamous, plural or celestial marriage association. But the people of Utah do not intend to so restrict themselves. The twelve or thirteen thousand heads of patriarchal or plural households are to be permitted to enjoy in the future, all the privileges resulting from their peculiar marriage status, and to harvest year by year, new crops of illegitimate children. It would seem that Congress owes a sacred duty to these children yet unborn. Further, by this instrument all polygamists are restored to the franchise. A conviction of bigamy or polygamy does not disqualify the convict as a voter, as the crime is not made a felony. [Sec. 1, Article 2.] The effect of participation in the political affairs of the State, by this large body of polygamists, may be easily imagined. Clearly, there is no evidence in this instrument of intention to make this class of offenses odious. In this immediate connection may properly be considered the declaration:

"SEC. 4, ART. 1: The right to worship God according to the dictates of conscience shall never be infringed; nor shall the State make any law respecting an establishment of religion or prohibiting the free exercise thereof; nor shall any control or interference with the rights of conscience be permitted."

The makers of this declaration have made conspicuous by their absence, the explanatory and qualifying provisos, which first appear in the colonial charter to Rhode Island, and are now contained in the Constitutions of the several States, i. e., that liberty of conscience so secured shall not be construed to excuse acts of licentiousness or justify practices inconsistent with the peace, good order, or safety of the State.

Reading this instrument between the lines, the reason of the omissions hereinbefore pointed out, is apparent.

If bigamy and polygamy are really intended, as defined in Section 12, Article 15, to include plural, patriarchal or celestial marriage, and the declaration of that section to voice the sentiment of the people, as being opposed to all forms and kinds of marriage except the monogamous relation, naturally one would expect to find in the instrument, a condemnation of acts which are universally decried as licentious and inconsistent with the good order, etc., of the State. We find no such condemnation, but on the contrary do find the emphatic announcement that no interference with the rights of conscience shall be permitted.

What rights of conscience are referred to is left for future construction. We do know, however, that the entire Mormon people (who are to administer this law if Statehood is granted) deem the right to take and live with many wives, as one of the dearest and most sacred rights of conscience. Here, then, is the true construction of section 12, article 15 and section 4, article 1: "No man may commit bigamy or polygamy, as we define those offences, but every true believer in the church, who obeys the revelation and enters into patriarchal, plural or celestial marriage, is not within the law, and as he believes the principle of such marriage to be a doctrine of religious faith, may live with his wives, and no control or interference with his right of conscience in this regard shall be permitted." If this is not the true intent of this instrument, we ask, why is it that the language of the Congressional Act of 1882, is not followed?

To avoid all quibbles, Congress found it necessary to define in terms the particular kinds of marriage prohibited. And why, were not the words "patriarchal" "plural" or "celestial," which have a settled significance· and meaning in Utah, employed in the definition of the offense? Was it because of the intention to make the distinction hereinbefore adverted to? Another significant fact presents itself in this connection. Granting for the sake of the argument that section 12, article 15, will be construed to include Mormon plural or celestial

marriages, it must be remembered that these are sol-
emnized in the temples, and as the evidence given in
the courts here shows, without witnesses. The difficulty in obtaining evidence of the marriage would be
so great as to practically result in defeating the operation of the law. Again, there is nothing to prevent the
legislature from so framing the rules of evidence in
such cases, as to render prosecutions useless. By requiring record evidence of, or the testimony of eye-witnesses
to, the first marriage, and by making the plural or polygamous wife an incompetent witness, the Constitutional
provision would be made ineffectual. It must be borne
in mind that we are not dealing with a people who are
friendly to legislation of this kind. The entire mass of
the community is hostile to it, and whether its prohibi-
tions are found in organic law or legislative act, we may
expect to find, in the future as in the past, the people
negatively, at least, opposing their enforcement. The
difficulties adverted to, cannot be overestimated. The
history of the courts in the Territory emphasizes the
suggestions here made. In the twenty years interven-
ing between the enactment of the first anti-polygamy
law and the passage of the Edmunds bill, (1882) there
was one conviction for polygamy. During the past
three years, while the Government was using every
effort with money and willing and zealous officers, to
enforce its laws, just *four* convictions for polygamy were
obtained. On the other hand, hundreds of men were
sentenced for unlawful cohabitation. The reason for
this difference is plain. A man commits polygamy in
the secret chambers of the temple, into which no pro-
fane may enter. The only witnesses are the high
priests who officiate, who are bound by solemn vows
against disclosures. The Government may prove that
the man entered the temple, but it cannot prove the
marriage. Ordinary prudence and circumspection will
enable the offenders to elude the officers until the

expiration of three years, the period of limitation. On the other hand, it is comparatively easy to make the proof required to convict for unlawful cohabitation. The association of a man with more than one woman as his wives, of necessity has some publicity about it. It gets out of doors, and is seen and observed by the world.

So also the failure to define the property rights of wives and to provide for their protection has its peculiar significance. Under the Constitution, women have no rights men are bound to respect; neither right of dower nor interest in the community property is provided for. This is in accordance with the policy of the Mormon Church. During all the years of its existence and power, it has strengthened its polygamous hand, by ignoring all distinction between lawful and unlawful wives,subjecting all alike so far as property rights were concerned, to the caprices of the male head of the household. With no rights in the property of the husband, save those he chooses to give her, the first wife, with her children, is practically at his mercy. He may abandon her for another, or he may coerce her *consent* (?) to his second or other marriage, and when the end comes, may leave her in her age to poverty and want, while the younger and fairer additions to his establishment succeed to all his temporal wealth.

The Congress of the United States should consider well this question. But yesterday it deemed it necessary for the protection of women in Utah, to grant the dower right to them. It was thought, and rightly, that it was one of the means for the regeneration of the Territory. It may be said that the regulation of property rights of women is peculiarly within the province of the local sovereignty, and that every State must determine such questions for itself. This is true as a general rule, but we are considering now the *good faith* of the people seeking a State Government, and in the light of their history, may judge of the *purpose* of these omissions.

Again, there is no guaranty in this instrument of
the freedom of speech and of the press.

SEC. 11, Article 1. The provision is, that the State
shall pass no law abridging the freedom of speech or
of the press. This is all. There is no declaration that
the citizen may speak, write and publish his sentiments on all subjects, being responsible only for the
abuse of that right; nor that the *truth* may be given
in evidence in civil and criminal suits as a defense.

If it were intended to leave it open for the Legislature, by enactment, to restore the law of libel as it
was when the great oratory of Erskine awakened the
conscience of all England, the result has been accomplished. Note here, the provisions relative to courts
and juries.

"SECTION 1, Article 6: The judicial power is to be vested in a Supreme,
Circuit, and such *inferior* courts as shall be established by law."

"SEC. 5, Article 1: The right of trial by jury still remains inviolate;
except that in the *inferior* courts a *number less than twelve* may constitute
a jury."

"SEC. 6, Article 6: The Legislature may confer limited *common law*
and chancery jurisdiction on *inferior* courts."

Here we have the authority for the erection by the
Legislature of special tribunals, which may sit with
juries of less than twelve. The judges thereof will be
creatures of the Legislature, and dependent on it for
their tenures and emoluments. Such tribunals, without Constitutional restraint, might be made terrible en-
gines of oppression, should the ecclesiastical power
deem it necessary to prevent all hostile criticism of its
creed or acts. It is idle to assume, that in Utah the
Church will not dominate the State. There will be no
State, it will be all Church.

The declaration (Sec. 3, Article 1) against the union
of Church and State, has but little weight, in view of
the fact that it is made by a community of one hundred and fifty thousand people, who assert as an article of their faith. that they are a people set apart by

God, for the accomplishment of a great divine purpose, to which end they must yield implicit obedience to their elders and priests, in temporal as well as spiritual affairs, and who believe that they are in direct and actual communication with the Almighty, and that He directs their affairs by revelation.

Remember that this people is made up largely of men and women of alien birth, who, impelled by superstition, sought Utah, not as an asylum where they could worship God according to their own consciences, but as the place of His Kingdom. They came here to aid in "building up the kingdom," and in the full belief that in time. they, His chosen people, shall govern the temporal affairs of earth. This is the one great object, (as the people are taught and believe,) of the "gathering of the Saints in these valleys." The promises of their revelation convince them that all who have been faithful and loyal to the church in this work. will reap the promised reward, that is to say, the men will all be kings, and the women queens in the life to come. They have never breathed the air of freedom, and have no idea of allegiance to the common country. Everything is subordinated to a creed, which with remorseless power has bound the fetters of its superstition about the brains of its devotees.

It is the spirit of loyalty to their faith. which prompts men, day by day, to refuse to promise to obey the laws of the land. When we we see men, by hundreds, refusing to take the oaths prescribed by law, and thereby disqualifying themselves as jurors and voters; when we find them going to prison by scores, rather than indicate their intentions to live within the law, when we hear such persons commended and extolled from every Mormon pulpit in Utah, as martyrs to the cause of *religious liberty*; when ostracism and persecution await and follow the man who *dares* to announce his intention of yielding obedience to the laws of his country; when we ascertain that there are Church tribunals, which have jurisdiction to determine questions of property and status, between all members of the organization, and whose decrees are held to be of more binding force than the judgments of the judicial courts; may we not conclude that the leaven of ecclesiastical power is working among the people, and that the declaration there shall be no union of Church and State, is full of sound but contains no substance?

Can we doubt that when such a people are freed from the restraints of Federal power, all their laws and methods of procedure, will be made to conform to the injunction of the Almighty as the same is *revealed* through the priest? And are the people of the United States willing to commit the lives, liberties and properties of thousands of their fellow citizens to the keeping of a majority, which has surrendered its conscience and thought to its religious teachers, who hold a power in temporal affairs, unparalleled in history.

Are they ready now to lay the foundations for a State, in the very heart of the Republic, which in its people and institutions, will be alien to every principle of American Government, antagonistic to real religious liberty, and hostile to all intellectual development?

There are many other objectionable features in the instrument under consideration, which clearly indicate the hand of the church. It is impossible in the limits of this article to enumerate, much less discuss them. A careful comparison made with the Constitution of Nevada, which is claimed to be the source of Utah's inspiration, will demonstrate the fact that very many of the provisions inserted for the protection of the State, are carefully and with discrimination eliminated here. Prominent among those, is the prohibition against perpetuities. Neither do we find any kind of declaration in the Utah instrument against the unlimited accumulation of property by the Church. In this particular this people is not in accord with the spirit of the age, which deems

the gathering of large amounts of property into the
dead hand as inimical to free institutions and the best
interests of society.

In conclusion, it may be said, that it will be easy
for the people of Utah to show their good faith and hon-
esty of purpose. If it be true that they have experienced
a change of heart, and are now animated by a desire to
bring the Territory on to the plane of a higher and better civilization, such faith and purpose may be easily
manifested. Every member of the convention which
framed the constitution is a member of the priesthood,
and nearly every one has been returned by the people
to the Legislature, which is to convene in January next.

Let these gentlemen enact a system of laws for
their people, which will *evidence* their intent to put the
past behind them. Let them say, by appropriate enactment, that cohabitation with more than one woman,
whether under the guise of marriage or not, and the,
consequent bringing of bastard children into the world,
is a *crime* against society, deserving the severest of punishment. Let them say, that the wife who gives her
virginity, her youth and her age to the husband of her
choice, must be honored and protected, not only by
him, but by the *State*.

Let them also provide by proper laws against the
encroachments of ecclesiastical power, and thus show
their independence of the priests who gave them their
places, and then let all the people cheerfully obey the
laws so enacted, and aid to enforce them. When these
things are done, it will be time enough to consider the
question of Statehood. Until some sort of understanding and recognition of duties which they owe to themselves and the people ot the United States, are manifested by the people of Utah, and such understanding
and recognition finds prominent place in their proposed organic law, the well-being and safety of the
country require that they should still remain subject
to Federal authority.

CONCLUSION.

The above is the situation in Utah as seen by the most eminent men of the Territory, and they give their opinions after long years of observation. It will be seen that the movement for Statehood is a direct fraud, that could it be carried through it would be the consummation of the monstrous crime of surrounding a Theocratic government, a government opposed in all things to this Republic, with the defenses of Statehood. The spirit of that Theocracy has not changed in the least since it was intolerable to the men of Missouri and Illinois. The seeming concessions are made simply because of the stress which the laws are bringing upon the illegal practices of the Mormon people, and their prayer for Statehood is simply a struggle to obtain the power to follow their own devices and to defy the Republic's sovereignty. For Congress to listen to their appeal would be the crime of the century.

The following paragraph from the decision of the Supreme Court of Utah Territory in the case of the United States vs. the the Church of Jesus Christ of Latter-day Saints may appropriately close this case:

This corporation, at the time of its organization, embraced nine-tenths of the inhabitants of the Territory,—many thousands of people. At the present time it includes probably more than 120,000, and if, in the future, people should continue to be gathered in from all quarters of the globe as they have in the past, their number at no distant day will reach a quarter of a million. The corporation extends over the whole Territory, including numerous congregations in various localities. At the head of this corporate body according to the faith professed, is a seer and revelator, who receives in revelation the will of the Infinite God concerning the duty of man to himself, to his fellow-beings, to society, to human government, and to God. In subordination to this head are a vast number of officers of various kinds and descriptions, comprising a most minute and complete organization. The people comprising this organization claim to be directed and led by inspiration that is above all human wisdom, and subject to a power above all municipal government,—above all " man-made laws." These facts belong to history, therefore we have taken notice of them,

www.ingramcontent.com/pod-product-compliance
Lightning Source LLC
Chambersburg PA
CBHW031447270326
41930CB00007B/904